KU-794-943

A Strategy for Justice

DISPOSED OF BY LIBRARY HOUSE OF LORDS

LEGAL ACTION GROUP (LAG) was founded in 1971 to improve legal services. It seeks to do this both through the provision of accessible information on the law and practice relevant to legal aid practitioners and lay advisers and by contributing to debate on how legal services should be delivered. LAG, which currently has over 1,000 members, publishes a monthly journal, *Legal Action*, a range of books and provides training courses. Further information can be obtained by writing to the Legal Action Group, 242 Pentonville Road, London N1 9UN.

A Strategy for Justice
Publicly funded legal services in the 1990s

Legal Action Group

LAG Legal Action Group
1992

This edition published in Great Britain 1992
by LAG Education and Service Trust Limited
242 Pentonville Road, London N1 9UN

© Legal Action Group, 1992

All rights reserved. No part of this publication may be reproduced, stored in a retrieval system or transmitted in any form or by any means, without permission from the publisher.

British Library Cataloguing in Publication Data

A CIP catalogue record for this book is available from the British Library.

ISBN 0 905099 37 0

Phototypeset by Kerrypress Ltd, Luton
Printed by The Cromwell Press, Melksham

Preface

In 1992, for the first time, central government spending on legal and advice services for the public will rise to over £1 billion. The Lord Chancellor has stated his intention to restrict the future growth of legal aid expenditure. Solicitors, concerned about levels of remuneration, have been incensed by government plans to extend payment by fixed fees – some have even withdrawn from duty solicitor schemes in protest. As a result of this conflict, public discussion has largely focused on only one issue: public expenditure versus remuneration of legal aid practitioners.

A far more fundamental question needs to be asked if legal services policy is to be placed on a rational basis. Why should public funding of legal services be a priority? The answer is simple. These services provide an important counterbalance to the evident inequalities in society, thereby helping to secure equal access to justice for all citizens.

Although such a goal must justify the commitment of public funds, expenditure should not necessarily be allocated in its current form. Two significant changes would help to provide a more rational policy. First, services need to be shaped to the requirements of their consumers, rather than to those of providers. Such an approach entails placing more emphasis on information and education than is currently the case, and the better integration of advice services with those available for litigation and representation. Second, services should be planned and co-ordinated, providing access throughout the country. The current position – in which the distribution of solicitors' offices and advice agencies is dictated by market forces and the vagaries of local authority generosity and solvency – is self-evidently unsatisfactory.

Different needs may require different forms of service. In LAG's view, private practitioners should remain as the major providers of criminal, family or personal injury representation. However, the development of salaried services, along the lines of law centres, would be more appropriate for areas of social welfare law and tribunal representation. Overall, a broader approach to reform necessitates considering legal services, legal procedures and substantive law as an integrated whole.

While LAG proposes areas where the transfer of resources could benefit consumers, it does not recommend piecemeal savings in current expenditure to fund its proposals. To do so would contradict one of the main functions of the approach set out in this book: to provide a means for the coherent planning of legal services. This could ensure that any growth in expenditure is the result of a constructive policy decision, rather than the product of a budget spiralling out of control.

A Strategy for Justice seeks to widen debate about publicly funded legal services in the 1990s in the above terms. It is in four parts. The first sets out LAG's understanding of the current situation and its historical background. Part II contains four chapters which look at legal needs in specific areas – family disputes, personal injury, debt and employment. These chapters stress the integral nature of legal services. Crime has been deliberately excluded, for two reasons. LAG's long-standing argument that areas of civil law – in particular, neglected aspects of social welfare law – need to be given higher priority is, with the possibility of cuts, even more urgent. Also, LAG's views on the criminal justice system have been submitted to the Royal Commission headed by Lord Runciman, and have been covered in the press and elsewhere. Part III examines legal service delivery in four foreign jurisdictions and draws certain lessons. The chapters in Part IV set out LAG's recommendations.

This book, the result of a study financed by the Nuffield Foundation, seeks to widen discussion before wrong decisions are taken on too narrow a view of the issues which are at stake in the future of publicly funded legal services.

Roger Smith, director, Legal Action Group
London, August 1992

Acknowledgements

The Legal Action Group gratefully acknowledges the assistance given in the preparation of this book by the following people: Lee Bridges, Carlos Dabezies, Duncan Forbes, Cyril Glasser, Professor Carol Harlow, who are all existing or former members of the LAG committee, Pat Thomas, deputy director of the Nuffield Foundation, Tamara Goriely, who was employed as a researcher during the first phase of the project and wrote early drafts of some of the chapters in parts 1 and 2, Roger Smith, director of LAG, who co-ordinated and wrote much of the book, and Hilary Arnott of LAG's editorial staff. LAG is also grateful to innumerable people who contributed in various other ways. Special thanks are also due to the help given by Nick Huls in the Netherlands, Stephanie Thomas in Ontario, Jacques Frémont in Quebec, and Rhonda Fadden, Terry Purcell, Richard Mitchell and Barbara Shalit in Australia.

LAG expresses its thanks to the Nuffield Foundation which funded the project.

Contents

Part I

Justice for all?

CHAPTER 1

Development since 1945

The current organisation and state of publicly funded legal services in England and Wales cannot be understood without some reference to the history of legal aid, law centres and advice agencies since the second world war. This history can be divided into three distinct periods: the first characterised as a period of foundation, the second as one of expansion and the third as one of stagflation.

- The first period encompassed the establishment and gradual evolution of the legal aid scheme. It began in 1945 with the publication of the report of the Rushcliffe Committee on Legal Aid and Legal Advice[1] and extended, quite precisely, until 17 July 1970, the formal opening date of the country's first law centre in London's North Kensington.
- The middle period, from 1970 to 1986, saw a massive expansion of all forms of publicly funded legal services. Legal aid increased in both scope and cost; law centres emerged and the advice sector re-established itself after a post-war decline. In January 1986, the police station duty solicitor scheme, the last major expansion of legally aided services, was put on the statute book.
- The final period, extending from 1986 until today, has seen a major challenge to the fundamental structure of publicly funded legal services. The spring of 1986 saw cuts to dependants' eligibility levels for legal aid and then, in the summer, an efficiency scrutiny which advocated the transfer of legal advice from solicitors to advice agencies. Since then, although the cost of legal aid has escalated and the numbers of people assisted have risen, eligibility for many matters covered by civil legal aid has fallen, local authority funding has been restricted and levels of professional remuneration are now causing concern, particularly to solicitors.

3

Setting up the legal aid scheme: 1945-70

The foundation stone of post-war public legal services was the report of the Rushcliffe committee. Its main recommendations were:

- Legal aid should be available in those types of cases where lawyers normally represented private individual clients.
- Legal aid should not be limited to people 'normally classed as poor', but should also include those of 'small or moderate means' (eligibility on income grounds covered about 80 per cent of the population when the legal aid scheme was established in 1950).
- There should be an increasing scale of contributions payable by those with income or capital above minimum levels, below which legal aid would be free.
- In addition to a means test, cases should be subject to a test of merit, designed to be judged by legal practitioners (not by the government or a government-appointed agency), on a basis similar to that applied to private clients.
- Legal aid should be funded by the state but administered by the Law Society. The Lord Chancellor should be the minister responsible, assisted by an advisory committee.
- Means investigation of applicants should be undertaken by the National Assistance Board (the forerunner of the Benefits Agency of the Department of Social Security).
- Barristers and solicitors acting under legal aid should receive 'adequate' remuneration.

Most of the committee's proposals were implemented. Some, however, were not. Legal aid is still not available for coroners' courts, although this was recommended. The committee also argued for a national, salaried advice service to supplement the work of private practitioners.

The committee's report represented an almost complete acceptance of the views of the Law Society. The Society wanted a full legal aid scheme – not least, because it was concerned that its members would find it difficult to re-establish their practices after the war. In particular, it wanted to wind down the salaried divorce department which it had established during the war. This represented too great a threat to the private practice model. In return for retaining considerably more control of its members' destiny than was, for example, being offered to the medical profession in the newly proposed National Health Service, the Society offered a discount of 15 per cent on fees charged for legal aid work.

In accepting the Law Society scheme, the Rushcliffe committee specifically rejected various alternatives that had been placed before it. Out went the Haldane Society's plans to base legal aid on the thousand or so newly created citizens' advice bureaux. Ignored also was the submission of the Poor Man's Lawyer Associations (lawyers who gave advice from the university-based settlements such as Toynbee Hall in the East End of London), which had called for greater priority to be given to work with the Rent Restriction Acts, and also for workmen's compensation, small claims and hire purchase. These areas, which played no part in the average solicitor's practice, were hardly touched on by the legal aid scheme until the early 1970s.

In US jargon, the civil legal aid scheme was, and is, a 'judicare' system, whereby representation is provided by private practitioners paid by public funds. The intention was to provide the same representation for low-income litigants that they would have obtained if they could afford a lawyer.

At least three internal factors, in addition to the obvious restrictions of eligibility criteria for clients and remuneration levels for lawyers, have limited expenditure on the scheme. First, an unsuccessful litigant is generally required by the courts to pay at least some of the costs of the successful party. This reduces the cost to the legal aid fund in cases where legally aided clients win. Second, the fund has first call on any damages or realisable financial assets which have been the subject of legally aided litigation to meet any outstanding costs. In effect, this 'statutory charge' means that legal aid represents a grant of money to a litigant who is unsuccessful, but a loan to one who wins. The third limiting factor has been the scope of the scheme. Initially, it was restricted to High Court civil matters. In 1960, it was expanded to the county court (the lower civil court). At the same time, legal aid became available for criminal cases in the magistrates' courts.

The Law Society's 1969/70 annual report provides a picture of how the scheme was working at the close of this first period (excluding legal aid in the higher criminal courts, which is funded separately).[2]

Law Society administration	£2m
Civil legal aid	£6m
Criminal (magistrates' courts)	£2m
Criminal (higher courts)	£4m
Total net cost	£14m

The costs of criminal legal aid in the magistrates' courts were still relatively low. They had, however, increased by 53 per cent over the figure for the previous year, reflecting the beginning of a period of deliberately increased availability following publication of the Widgery report on criminal legal aid in 1966.[3] Family law accounted for the vast majority of civil expenditure – a 1969 survey of legal aid certificates in Birmingham found that only 9 per cent were for accident claims and under 5 per cent for other problems; the rest concerned family matters.[4]

The end of this period saw one other extension of legal aid – to the Lands Tribunal, which deals with certain property rights. In its 1969/70 annual report, the Lord Chancellor's Advisory Committee on Legal Aid argued for more attention to be given to the needs of people appearing before tribunals and called for 'some form of ancillary legal services'. However, the Lands Tribunal remains one of the few tribunals in which legal aid is available.

An emerging challenge

In the late 1960s, the legal aid scheme began to come under pressure from an alternative model of publicly funded legal services, influenced by developments in the United States. There, legal challenge had played an important part in the civil rights movement; legal services also came to be seen as an integral part of President Johnson's 'war on poverty'.

The first director of the US Legal Services Corporation, Clinton Bamberger, articulated the explicitly political belief of a generation of radical lawyers in the US: 'Our responsibility is to martial the forces of law and the strength of lawyers to combat the causes and effects of poverty. Lawyers must uncover the legal causes of poverty, remodel the systems which generate the cycle of poverty and design new social, legal and political tools and vehicles to move poor people from deprivation, depression and despair to opportunity, hope and ambition.'[5]

This was heady stuff. The US experience filtered into Britain, given a major boost by two political pamphlets.[6] The Society of Labour Lawyers' *Justice for All* was published in December 1968. An appendix described the work of the US 'neighbourhood law firms' and the pamphlet argued for an extension of this model into Britain. In the same month, the Committee of Conservative Lawyers published its own proposals in *Rough Justice*. Though considerably less radical, this argued for more planning of legal aid so that, for instance, private practitioners would be encouraged by special additional payments to set up in poor areas.

Several other currents contributed to a more activist approach to legal services in the late 1960s. There was a flowering of political action; community-based groups sprang up; sociologists were 'rediscovering' poverty; and an expanding higher education system was enabling a broader range of students to encounter law. A gathering movement of law students, academics and practising lawyers, highly critical of the conservatism of the legal profession and the limitations of the legal aid scheme, became involved in various forms of informal legal advice provision. For example, the law centre in North Kensington evolved from advice sessions, begun in 1967 and linked to a community group, the Notting Hill People's Association.

This critical movement had sufficient strength to force some measure of official recognition. The Lord Chancellor asked his legal aid advisory committee to respond to the two pamphlets. Its report, published in January 1970, was strongly influenced by a submission from the Law Society[7] arguing for a new and flexible legal advice scheme and for the establishment of law centres to be transferred to its control. These recommendations were repeated by the committee.

Expanding legal services: 1970–86

Between 1970 and 1986, legal aid expanded, both in its range of schemes and in expenditure. In 1973, the Law Society got its advice and assistance scheme, generally known as the 'green form' scheme, whereby advice on any matter of English law was available on the basis of a simplified test of income and expenditure carried out by the solicitor. In 1982, legal representation at mental health review tribunals became available through ABWOR (assistance by way of representation), a variant of the green form scheme. The Law Society also gradually expanded its duty solicitor schemes in the magistrates' courts. Initially, these were voluntary, but, from 1 January 1984, they were given a statutory basis. Then, in 1986, under the auspices of the Police and Criminal Evidence Act 1984, duty schemes were statutorily established for advice in police stations.

The cost of the legal aid fund administered by the Law Society (ie, excluding legal aid in the higher criminal courts) grew from £8 million in 1969/70 to £265 million in 1986/87.[8] In 1986, total payments to the legal profession under all forms of legal aid was £419 million; the net cost to the Exchequer (excluding client contributions and other costs recovered) was £342 million. The cost of criminal legal aid, which in the mid to late 1970s had risen to 60 per cent of total legal aid costs, was still running at over half of the budget. Most significantly, the share of legal aid going on criminal cases in the magistrates' courts had doubled since 1969/70, accounting for one-quarter of all legal aid costs in 1986/87.

The rise in the absolute cost of legal aid was reflected in its increasing importance to the legal profession. For solicitors, legal aid represented about 6 per cent of their total fees in 1975/76; in 1985/86 it was almost 11 per cent.[9] The Bar's dependence – estimated at around 30 per cent in 1977 by the Royal Commission on Legal Services[10] – was much greater: just over one-fifth of its total income came from criminal legal aid.[11] Thus, legal aid helped to fund a major expansion of both branches of the profession in the 1970s and 1980s: between 1971 and 1981, the Bar grew from 2,714 members to 4,685; the number of solicitors grew from 25,366 to 39,795 over the same period.[12]

Various forces lay behind this expansion. Criminal work increased massively as representation in the magistrates' courts became the norm: in 1969, only one in five of defendants appearing on an indictable offence in magistrates' courts was represented under legal aid; by 1986, the figure had risen to an all-time high of over four-fifths. Another influence was a soaring divorce rate: in 1968, the divorce rate stood at 3.7 per 1,000 marriages; by 1972, two years after the Divorce Reform Act 1969 came into force, it had risen to 9.4 per 1,000 and, by 1986, it had reached 12.9 per 1,000.[13] Legal aid for divorce itself was withdrawn in 1977, but the number of 'ancillary applications' relating to maintenance and children continued to rise (see chapter 3).

Another factor was the dramatic increase in eligibility for civil legal aid introduced by the Labour government just before it lost office in 1979. From an initial 80 per cent of the population in 1950, eligibility on income grounds had slumped to 40 per cent by 1973. From this low point, eligibility on income grounds was increased to 79 per cent of the population in 1979.[14]

The green form legal advice scheme had been advocated by the Law Society as a way of encouraging solicitors into the fields of welfare law pioneered by the law centres. In fact, it was used largely to finance work in traditional fields of activity – crime and family. Between them, these accounted for half of the bills paid out in 1985/86. The slow move into welfare law is shown by the figures below. Although these indicate a growth over ten years from 27,000 to 172,000 of green forms attributable to the 'social welfare law' areas (landlord and tenant, employment, hire purchase and debt, welfare benefits and consumer), expressed as a percentage of all green forms, this represented only a rise from 10.7 per cent to 17.3 per cent.

Percentage of all green form bills paid

	1975/76	1980/81	1985/86
Landlord and tenant	4.7	4.8	5.6
Employment	1.5	2.2	2.0
HP and debt	3.4	2.8	5.0
Welfare benefits*	1.1	1.6	2.1
Immigration and nationality	n/a	0.5	0.7
Consumer	n/a	1.4	1.9
Percentage of total	10.7	13.3	17.3
Total number of all green forms	253,172	531,512	1,038,805

*The category heading varied over the years but, substantially, the work covered welfare benefits.

Law centres win acceptance

The Law Society hoped to control the emergent law centres by the conditions it attached to 'waivers' (special permission granted by the Society and required by solicitors employed in law centres) from the professional rules then existing against advertising and sharing fees. In its 1973/74 report on the legal aid scheme, the Society criticised law centres' ideas of 'responsibility to their local communities' as 'stirring up political and quasi-political confrontation far removed from ensuring equal access to the protection of the law'.[15]

By 1975, the Law Society had worked itself into a position where it acceded to pressure from a group of solicitors in Hillingdon, West London, who were outraged by the imminent funding of a local law centre. It tried to stop solicitors practising in the centre by refusing them the necessary waivers, on the ground that local solicitors met local need for services. The subsequent political impasse resulted in the intervention of the Labour Lord Chancellor, Lord Elwyn Jones, and the Society was threatened with legislation to overcome its resistance.

The Law Society and the law centres eventually reached an accommodation, negotiated under pressure from the Lord Chancellor, with assistance from the Legal Action Group as mediator, that suited both. Provided that the law centres did not compete with private practice in its traditional areas – such as adult crime, matrimonial work, personal injury, probate and conveyancing – the Society would grant the necessary permission. By the time of its evidence to the Royal Commission on Legal Services in 1979, the Society had come round to the view that, far from being a threat, law centres generated work for private practice.

The second half of the 1970s then saw a flowering of the law centre movement. A major source of funds came from the various schemes for inner-city rejuvenation, involving a partnership between local authorities and the Department of the Environment. In 1975, the Lord Chancellor also instituted central government funding of a small number of centres which were in financial difficulties.

By 1986, the number of law centres in England and Wales stood at 55. However, further growth in the 1980s had been stunted by a drying up of funds. The initial grant from the Lord Chancellor's Department was never extended to other law centres, and, in 1982, they ceased to be a priority for central funding from inner city programmes. The government took the view that law centre funding, though desirable, was a matter for local government.

During this period, non-lawyer advice services also flourished. Citizens' advice bureaux, established during the second world war but thereafter neglected for some years, re-established themselves. Between 1966 and 1986, their numbers almost doubled (from 473 to 869) and the annual volume of enquiries more than quadrupled (from 1.3 million to 6.8 million).[16] In addition, several hundred independent advice centres were set up, many of which grew out of community action projects. There was also a gradual development of largely local authority-funded specialist services, giving advice on housing, social security and debt.

In the 1970s, the CAB service experimented with the employment of solicitors. The first combined CAB and law centre opened in Paddington in 1973, followed by a similar venture in Hackney in 1976. Community lawyers, who both advised on individual problems and trained lay advisers within the bureaux, were appointed to CABx in North Kensington, Lewisham and Waltham Forest. By 1977, ten CABx were employing lawyers and the National Association of CABx resolved to develop more posts.

The system under scrutiny: 1986–92

This final period, from 1986 to the present day, has been characterised by, on the one hand, increasing government concern to hold down the growth in legal aid expenditure and, on the other, a struggle against a general retrenchment in the funding of public legal and advice services. The first major sign of a cost-reducing approach occurred in the spring of 1986, when, in a panic measure to keep costs down, legal aid eligibility allowances for dependants were cut. Then, in the summer, the government instituted a legal aid efficiency scrutiny.[17] This was conducted in the then fashionable style of a rapid review, timed to last around a hundred days, by three junior civil servants. Its recommendation that large areas of the green form legal advice and assistance scheme be transferred to the voluntary advice sector represented the first government-led challenge to the legal profession's dominance over all forms of legal aid.

In the event, after fierce debate, the recommendation was scuppered. The CAB service, although initially tempted, eventually refused to co-operate. The scrutiny resulted in only minor cuts to the green form scheme in relation to wills. But the agenda for more government intervention was set.

The Legal Aid Act 1988 demonstrated this. The new legislation transferred the Law Society's administrative roles, which covered all legal aid except the Crown Court, to a newly created Legal Aid Board. No less than half the initial membership of the board came from business, while the role of the Law Society was reduced to putting forward the names of two solicitors. Simultaneously, the calculation of legal aid remuneration at a discounted market rate was abolished. Henceforth, the level of remuneration was, effectively, left to the mercy of the Lord Chancellor.

Two further developments in this period had an indirect effect on legal aid. In 1988, the report of a comprehensive review of civil justice, instigated by the previous Lord Chancellor, Lord Hailsham, was published.[18] Implementation of its recommendations has caused cases to be transferred down the civil court system, increasing the jurisdiction of the small claims procedure in the county court, for which legal aid is not available. Then, in 1989, Lord Hailsham's successor, Lord Mackay, issued a green paper on the future of the legal profession.[19] The effect of legislation arising from this is discussed in the next chapter.

An impending sense of crisis in legal aid for the legal profession, primarily among solicitors, has been engendered by successive speeches of Lord Mackay, particularly since the autumn of 1991. With 1991/92 legal aid expenditure looking set to run over its budget estimate by more than £200 million, and 1992/93 expenditure likely to exceed £1 billion for the first time, Lord Mackay faces pressures to stem this rapid increase. In September 1991, he warned that 'resources are finite'; then, two weeks later, he announced: 'We are just about at the limit of what is possible without radical change.'[20] In furtherance of such 'radical change', his department had published proposals in the previous June for the reform of civil legal aid in which it introduced the idea of a 'safety net', whereby many litigants would have to begin their cases on a private basis before becoming entitled to legal aid.[21] However, the Legal Aid Board rejected the plan as 'too complicated and too burdensome',[22] and implementation now looks unlikely. The proposals in Part IV of this book are designed to provide a more co-ordinated and thorough approach to reform.

References

1   *Report of the Committee on Legal Aid and Legal Advice in England and Wales* Cmd 6641, HMSO, 1945 (Rushcliffe committee).
2   *Legal Aid and Advice: report of the Law Society and recommendations of the Lord Chancellor's Advisory Committee 1969-70 [Twentieth Report]* HC 446, HMSO, 1971.
3   *Report of the Departmental Committee on Legal Aid in Criminal Proceedings* Cmnd 2934, HMSO, 1966.
4   L Bridges, B Sufrin, J Whetton, and R White *Legal Services in Birmingham* Birmingham University, 1975.
5   Quoted in J Handler, E Hollingsworth and H Erlanger *Lawyers and the Pursuit of Legal Rights* Academic Press Inc, 1978, p5.
6   Society of Labour Lawyers *Justice for All* Fabian Research Pamphlet No 273, 1968, and Society of Conservative Lawyers *Rough Justice* SCL, 1968.
7   *Report of the Advisory Committee on the Better Provision of Legal Advice and Assistance* HC 4229, HMSO, 1970.
8   *36th Annual Reports of The Law Society and the Lord Chancellor's Advisory Committee (1985-86)* HC 87, HMSO, 1986.
9   *Royal Commission on Legal Services Final Report (Benson commission)* Cmnd 7648, HMSO, 1979, Volume 1, para 36.81, and C Glasser, 'Financing legal services' *Law Society's Gazette* 20 April 1988.
10   As in 9, volume 1, para 36.47.
11   As in 9, volume 2, table 18.18.
12   R Abel *The Legal Profession in England and Wales* Blackwell, 1988, tables 1.16 and 2.14.
13   L Stone *Road to Divorce: England 1530-1987* Oxford University Press, 1990, Table 13.1, p436.
14   Lord Chancellor's Advisory Committee on Legal Aid *26th Legal Aid Annual Reports [1975-76]* HC 12, HMSO, 1976, p60; M Murphy *Legal Aid Eligibility: calculation and interpretation of recent trends* Legal Action Group, 1989, Table 7.

15 Legal Aid and Advice: Report of the Law Society and comments and recommendations of the Lord Chancellor's Advisory Committee 1973–1974 [twenty-fourth report] HC 20, HMSO, 1974, appendix 18, p40.

16 National Consumer Council The Fourth Right of Citizenship: a review of local advice services NCC, 1977, p11 and National Association of Citizens Advice Bureaux Annual Report 1986–1987 NACAB, 1987, (figures for 1986/87).

17 Legal Aid Efficiency Scrutiny Lord Chancellor's Department, June 1986.

18 Civil Justice Review Report of the Review Body on Civil Justice Cm 394, HMSO, 1988.

19 Lord Chancellor's Department The Work and Organisation of the Legal Profession Cm 570, HMSO, 1989.

20 Speeches 22 September 1991 and 4 October 1991.

21 Review of Financial Conditions of Legal Aid Eligibility for Civil Legal Aid: a consultation paper Lord Chancellor's Department, 1991.

22 Response to the Lord Chancellor's Consultation paper: review of financial conditions for legal aid – eligibility for civil legal aid Legal Aid Board, 1991, para 6.

CHAPTER 2

The current position

Current debate about publicly funded legal services has been dominated both by the government's concern over the cost of legal aid and by the legal profession's anxiety regarding its level of remuneration. Important as these are, a proper discussion about the future of these services demands an appraisal of several other significant issues too. This chapter offers LAG's analysis of the state of legal aid and of publicly funded legal services generally as they stood in the spring of 1992.

Rising costs

The cost of legal aid needs consideration. Lord Mackay, Lord Chancellor since 1987, complained in October 1991 to an audience of legal aid practitioners that, 'over the past ten years, the net costs of the legal aid scheme have increased each year by an average of 17 per cent and the cost of each act of assistance (excluding the duty solicitor schemes) by 11 per cent. In the same period, inflation increased by an average of 7 per cent each year and the gross domestic product by 9 per cent each year. One does not have to be a mathematician to recognise that such a high increase each year in the proportion of the national wealth spent on legal aid cannot continue indefinitely.'[1]

Legal aid costs are rising sharply, both overall and per case. The Lord Chancellor's Department must have been taken to task by Treasury ministers for expenditure which has jumped from £685 million in 1990/91 to an estimated outturn of £907 million for 1991/92 (excluding administration costs), particularly when the public estimate of expenditure for the latter was set at only £698 million as late as February 1991.[2]

Figures for the net cost of legal aid (ie, excluding contributions from clients and costs) in 1991/92 were:[3]

14

	£m
Criminal	
Higher courts	186
Magistrates' courts	210
Police station advice	54
Court duty solicitors	8
Civil	
Non-matrimonial	161
Matrimonial	115
Interim payments	52
ABWOR	22
Criminal and civil	
Legal advice	95
Administration	
Legal Aid Board	41
Total	944

The combined cost of all forms of criminal legal aid and advice was £472 million, representing 52 per cent of total net expenditure.

A detailed breakdown of bills paid for 1991/92 in respect of all legal aid administered by the Legal Aid Board (ie, excluding legal aid in the higher criminal courts) shows the distribution of work within the different schemes.

	Numbers of bills paid
Criminal: magistrates' courts	477,000
Criminal: police station advice	549,000
Criminal: duty solicitors (courts)	233,000
Civil: non-matrimonial	127,000
Civil: matrimonial/family	129,000
Civil: interim payments	230,000
Green form	1,230,000
ABWOR	66,000

The 1991/92 figures above represent a 36 per cent increase in bills paid for civil legal aid since 1987/88, an 8 per cent increase in ABWOR bills, a 14 per cent increase in green form bills and a 17 per cent increase in magistrates' court criminal legal aid. These figures are affected by factors such as the Legal Aid Board's efficiency in processing bills. However, there is no doubt that more people are using legal aid.

The Legal Aid Board is less concerned with the growth in expenditure resulting from increasing numbers of cases than with rises in the cost per case. It considers the latter in its latest annual report, which contains figures for the changing lengths of time spent on the different constituent parts of a criminal legal aid case, as recorded by solicitors in submitting their bills. These figures are more useful than the more generally used figure of percentage increases in cost, which is affected by such matters as changes in the rate of VAT. The table below, taken from a study by the board, shows the increases in the average time spent on criminal legal aid cases:

	1988 (hours)	1991 (hours)	% *increase*
Attendance	2.04	2.45	20
Preparation	1.28	1.86	44
Travel to hearing	1.30	1.42	9
	(numbers)	(numbers)	
Letters	7.3	8.9	22
Telephone calls	7.2	8.0	11

One cynical explanation of these figures is that solicitors may be extending the time that cases take in order to maximise their return and compensate for what they see as low annual inflation increases in their hourly rates. There may be some truth in this, but the accusation has been strongly resisted by the Law Society, which rejects the accuracy of the board's sample of cases. Indeed, some of the board's other data do not support the case for wholly blaming solicitors for the rise in cost. For instance, the average length of case between the first and last piece of work charged for has increased by almost one-quarter, indicating that cases may actually be taking longer, perhaps because of prosecution or court delays. Furthermore, solicitors are not, overall, spending more time on green form advice. Over the last ten years, the average time claimed by a solicitor in a green form bill has remained at around 1.6 hours, against a maximum for all but matrimonial cases (where the limit is 3) of 2 hours.

In its response to the efficiency scrutiny on legal aid, the Law Society suggested six reasons why expenditure has risen: the rise in divorces; increase in property ownership; rising crime and attention to law and order; increasing complexity in the law; rising unemployment causing increased eligibility for legal aid, more debt, family breakdown and homelessness, and a greater awareness of rights.[4] Each may have some validity.

The profession and legal aid

Legal aid is a significant source of income for the legal profession. The Law Society reported that, in 1990/91, solicitors received £571 million in legal aid and barristers £145 million.[5] For solicitors, this represented a 17.5 per cent increase on the previous year. Of the £5.2 billion turnover of all solicitors, legal aid contributed 11.1 per cent. This is roughly the same proportion as five years previously, but close to double the 6 per cent figure for 1975/76 reported to the Royal Commission on Legal Services (see p8). (In fact, the proportions are probably slightly lower than those given by the Law Society because its figures for legal aid include VAT and disbursements, while other sources of income do not.)

The Bar is rather more secretive than the Law Society about the total earnings of its members. However, figures released in 1989 showed an even greater dependence on legal aid and public funds. Legal aid then accounted for 27 per cent of the total fee income of all barristers[6] – a proportion similar to that given to the Royal Commission for Legal Services in 1977 (see p8).

These income figures suggest little change in the legal profession's involvement in legal aid over the last decade. The number of solicitors' offices recorded as receiving a legal aid payment in any one year has also remained roughly constant, at just over 11,000, for the last five years. The Law Society estimates that this represents a payment to 74 per cent of all offices, indicating that some legal aid work is still undertaken by a broad range of solicitors' practices.[7]

Within this overall pattern, however, there are significant variations. First, there are strong regional differences. In 1990/91, legal aid constituted only 3.2 per cent of the income of solicitors in London (including the City), but 19 per cent for solicitors in Merseyside and the North.[8] Second, there are signs that a separate group of specialist solicitors' offices undertaking large amounts of legal aid has emerged. In 1991/92, 1,555 solicitors' offices received £120,000 or more from the Legal Aid Board. Although these represented only 14 per cent of all offices receiving a legal aid payment, together they received 59 per cent of the money paid out by the board.

Legal aid has thus established itself as being of considerable importance to the legal profession. In 1988, however, the Law Society warned that, because of declining levels of remuneration, there was 'widespread concern that solicitors are ceasing to accept legal aid work or are seriously considering giving it up'.[9] It has repeated this warning since, but as yet solicitors do not appear to be giving up legal aid work in any significant numbers.

Legacies of Rushcliffe

The consequences of the Rushcliffe model of provision, which based legal aid on the existing pattern of legal practice, are still evident. One positive effect of this can be seen from comparison with the five foreign jurisdictions described in Part III. Legal aid in England and Wales is more favourably financed, particularly in relation to crime, than elsewhere. The demand-led nature of the legal aid budget, combined with the commercial drive of solicitors anxious to maximise income, has undoubtedly operated to defend legal aid from a level of cuts which might otherwise have been expected. The experience of Quebec (see chapter 9) suggests that a service highly dependent on salaried lawyers is vulnerable to a government wishing to hold down costs. Furthermore, lawyers in this country have managed to keep their remuneration rates from public funds significantly higher than in the other jurisdictions.

One of the consequences of widespread dependence on private practitioners has, however, been the large-scale neglect of social welfare law. Solicitors continue to use even the most flexible element of legal aid provision, the green form legal advice scheme, largely to subsidise their traditional pattern of work. A report commissioned by the Lord Chancellor's Department and published in 1988 confirmed that 'solicitors have not for the most part seized the opportunity under the green form scheme to develop interests outside those of traditional legal practice . . . It has been the Law Centres rather than private practice which have sought to use the green form scheme to cover issues outside mainstream legal practice.'[10]

In consequence, there has been little change in the pattern of green form use. The continuing domination of criminal, matrimonial and family work is clear. Among green form bills in 1991/92, about 20 per cent of cases related to crime and 35 per cent to matrimonial and family work. As for social welfare law, it still made up only 26 per cent of all green form bills paid. Although four of the five social welfare categories saw the highest increase in green form use – immigration and nationality was up 48 per cent on the previous year, welfare benefits 33 per cent, hire purchase and debt 29 per cent and employment 25 per cent – this was, in part, an effect of recession. In overall terms, the growth in social welfare law advice and assistance remains slow (see p9).

Percentage of all green form bills paid 1990/91

Landlord and tenant, housing	7.6
Employment	2.2
HP and debt	6.7
Welfare benefits	5.6
Immigration and nationality	1.9
Consumer	1.9
% of total	25.9

This low use of the scheme suggests that the unmet need for legal services – taken up as an issue in the 1960s and 1970s, but now unfashionable – should remain a matter of concern. The need for legal services in two social welfare areas, debt and employment, are considered in chapters 5 and 6.

Another example of need arises in the field of housing. A consultation paper issued by the Civil Justice Review in 1987 accepted a large measure of unmet need in relation to disrepair: 'The judicial statistics for 1985 show that non-possession housing cases numbered no more than 1,500 in that year, yet the English House Condition Survey undertaken by the Department of the Environment in 1981 shows that in that year 2,796,000 rented dwellings were each in need of repairs costing over £1,000. It is therefore a working assumption of this study that potentially many more than the 1,500 litigants a year might seek a remedy through the courts in respect of a non-possession housing claim.'[11] The research also indicated that, although 78 per cent of a small sample of potential litigants had consulted a CAB, none had been advised to take court action.

Tenants thus make little use of legal advice and litigation to solve problems such as housing disrepair. Subsequent research for the CAB service suggests that lay volunteer advisers are hard pressed to deal with such a complicated area of law. It concluded that 'housing advice falls short of an acceptable minimum standard in a substantial number of cases'.[12] In around half of the cases studied, tenants were referred only to the environmental health or housing department, although, in the view of the researchers, legal action was more likely to be effective.

Solicitors' widespread neglect of social welfare law has been paralleled by government indifference. There still remains no nationally financed scheme for representation in tribunals. Legal aid in one form or another is available only for relatively few hearings – as shown in the 1991/92 figures for bills paid in relation to mental health review tribunals (3,577), certain appeals relating to prisoners (116), and the employment appeal tribunal – really an appellate court (145). By default, advice agencies have provided some representation at tribunals, much of which is of high quality. In the area of social security, particular expertise has been developed, but research commissioned by the Lord Chancellor's Department found that it is still the case that only about one in five of those bringing a social security appeal receive any advice, and 'only 12 per cent of appellants at social security appeals tribunals are represented by agencies or individuals with experience of representation or with any special expertise'.[13] The research concluded that representation increased a claimant's chance of a favourable outcome, 'though representation provided by generalist sources of advice has a less pronounced effect on outcome overall than that of specialists'.[14] The need for tribunal representation also emerges strongly from the analysis of employment work in chapter 6.

The absence of planned provision

Legal aid is, on the whole, only available where solicitors choose, for commercial reasons, to provide it. The explosion of criminal legal aid has undoubtedly helped in encouraging a limited number of legal aid firms to establish themselves in the poorer areas of the inner cities worst provided for in the 1960s. There is, however, still an overwhelming tendency for criminal practitioners to base their offices near city centre courts. There is also a dearth of provision in rural areas. A study of Devon and Cornwall concluded that firms in country areas 'lack any obvious expertise in the less lucrative areas of social welfare law. There appears to be little pressure for solicitors in rural areas to seek to develop new sources of work.'[15]

Future developments may reduce the accessibility of legal aid even further. If the economy improves, financial institutions may make a further and more vigorous bid to undertake conveyancing. This would potentially affect the commercial viability of the traditional, mixed 'High Street' practice and accelerate the existing division of solicitors into those whose practices are based on commercial work, various types of 'niche' practices (such as copyright or entertainment specialists), and legal aid practitioners. The latter might then become inaccessible to people living in some suburban or rural areas.

The policies of the Legal Aid Board may be another factor in the encouragement of larger legal aid units. It has developed the idea of franchising – that is, making contracts with the larger providers of legal aid under which the board has more control of quality, in return for more decision-making delegated to the solicitors and the promise of quicker payment. Its original suggestion was that such franchises should only be available to those solicitors' offices with a legal aid turnover of £40,000 or more.

The delivery of publicly funded legal services cannot be left to the mechanisms of the market. There is a need to consider how services should be planned so that all members of society in all parts of the country have an acceptable level of access.

The divided profession

Legal aid has operated to sustain Britain's unique model of a divided legal profession. Of the two branches, the Bar receives proportionately higher funding from public funds. Its General Council estimated that, 'in 1989, barristers earned 10 per cent of fees earned by practising lawyers but 29 per cent of publicly funded fees'.[16] In fact, the total funding of the Bar from public funds was probably a higher percentage, since this 29 per cent appears to include only fees from the Legal Aid Board and the Crown Prosecution Service, and discounts income from other government sources, such as via the Government Legal Service or the Customs and Excise Department.

Even so, for barristers, legally aided work is relatively badly paid. In consequence, despite a professional duty to undertake legal aid cases recently imposed in the Bar's code of conduct, legally aided clients tend to be the first to suffer if any barrister has a conflict of commitments.[17] Briefs in uncontested or relatively small criminal cases are often returned to solicitors, with the result that legally aided clients may find that their representation is rearranged at the last moment.

The Courts and Legal Services Act 1990 provides the framework for solicitors to undertake work previously reserved for barristers. A recent report from the Lord Chancellor's Advisory Committee on Legal Education and Conduct recommended that solicitors in private practice should qualify for rights of audience in the higher courts.[18] Legally aided clients might benefit from implementation of this recommendation, particularly in criminal cases. The possible consequences of these changes are discussed further in chapter 14 (see p144).

Disparate provision

The provision of publicly funded legal services is divided in another way. While the legal aid scheme is historically based on, and still largely dominated by, the idea of funding litigation through lawyers, advice agencies have evolved from a very different background. In consequence, many advice agencies are orientated towards a model of advice, information and counselling ultimately derived from a nineteenth-century charitable model. In addition, some reflect an orientation stemming from an impetus in the 1960s and 1970s towards community action and development. In default of other provision, advice agencies have supplied much of the available assistance and representation in social welfare law. Unless the agencies happen to employ a lawyer (as very few of them do), they exist largely outside the legal aid system. Instead, like law centres, they are overwhelmingly dependent on grant aid from local authorities.

No central government department takes responsibility for the funding of advice agencies, and there is no central information on their total resources, though the CAB service provides information on itself. Core funding from all local authorities for CABx, which totalled £27.5 million in 1990/91, varies considerably. The National Association of Citizens Advice Bureaux reported that, for 1990/91, 'funding from county councils varied from nothing to close to £30,000; funding from metropolitan districts ranged from just over £30,000 to over £560,000'.[19] NACAB itself received a grant from the Department of Trade and Industry of £10.3 million. The Federation of Independent Advice Centres gets no core funding from central government, although it receives a number of individual grants, largely for management training.

The distribution of advice agencies is totally dependent on the funding available, making provision as uneven and unrelated to need as that provided by solicitors. Law centres, of which there were 57 in July 1992, are in a similar position.

The 1986 efficiency scrutiny report was the first enquiry into legal aid to look seriously at using the skills of advice centres. Its most controversial recommendations were that: 'except in criminal cases, initial advice should be given by an advice agency rather than a private practitioner. Family cases should be referred to a private practitioner once it is clear that there is an issue on which legal advice is needed, but other civil cases should be referred only when court proceedings need to be initiated.'[20] These evoked protest from both solicitors and advice agencies, who agreed that it represented an attempt to save money and reduce services. The idea of using the skills of advice agencies is a feature of the Legal Aid Board's experiment with franchising in Birmingham. Agencies could apply for franchises to carry out green form work alongside private firms. The board's annual report for 1991/92 reported that five advice agencies had been granted a franchise in one or more categories in its pilot project.[21] Incorporation of advice agencies within the legal aid system does, however, lead to potential problems. First, contracts do not help advice agencies to gain reliable core funding, and those under threat of closure are in no position to consider expanding to meet the contract conditions. Second, franchising expects advice agencies to provide the same service as solicitors, which ignores the special contribution of their accessible, non-legal and more pro-active approach.

Constraints on local authority funding are being felt throughout the voluntary sector, and a number of law centres have been subject to cuts. The London Borough of Wandsworth withdrew its funds in 1990; several other authorities – including Labour-controlled Brighton and Conservative-controlled Brent – have tried to diminish their law centres' separate identity by way of amalgamating them with their own advice agencies, at the same time placing restrictions on the work they do.

In a more positive light, NACAB was able to say in its annual report, 'it is gratifying that very few authorities decided to limit their grants to bureaux in 1990–91 despite their own internal funding problems'. Nevertheless, there have been closures and NACAB noted with concern 'the combination of community charge capping and a general squeeze on local authorities'. It reported the closure of two bureaux in 1990/91 – North Shields and Hampstead, north London.[22] Since then, at least two more, in Clapham and Balham in south London, have closed.

Independent advice agencies are as concerned as NACAB over their future, with FIAC members as diverse as Harlesden Advice Centre in the London borough of Brent and Ask Here, a young people's project in Birmingham, recently losing funds.

The proven unreliability of local government funding has encouraged both advice agencies and law centres to look for more consistent central government resources. The Law Centres Federation has promoted the idea of a nationally funded network of law centres (see p134). In its 1990/91 annual report, NACAB declared its support for a proposal that 'local authorities should have a statutory duty to plan for and fund advice services in their locality. This should be backed up by a clear recognition of advice needs in the Standing Spending Assessment',[23] against which local authority expenditure is measured by central government.

The fall in eligibility

Eligibility for civil legal aid and green form legal advice has fallen substantially from the levels to which it was raised just before the Labour government lost office in 1979. As late as 1986, this development was denied by the then Lord Chancellor, Lord Hailsham, who asserted that cuts in dependants' allowances would be 'practically unobservable' and reasserted that around 70 per cent of the population met the income criteria for grant of civil legal aid.[24]

Much of the debate about levels of eligibility has been conducted with regard to the proportion of the population eligible on grounds of income. No overall figures for eligibility can be given because the government produces no reliable statistics on savings and other matters relevant to eligibility under the capital criteria. The criteria, however, clearly operate to exclude significant numbers of otherwise eligible applicants.

The capital limits for green form, ABWOR and for most applicants for civil legal aid are now significantly lower than those for income support, whose recipients are automatically eligible for free legal aid. In effect, therefore, those not on income support face more stringent capital limits for legal aid than those receiving income support. The limits are also out of line with the figure for housing benefit or community charge, a comparable form of assistance for those on low incomes. The result is a completely illogical system.

An indication that levels of eligibility are falling is given by the decline in the proportion of civil legal aid certificates for which the assisted person is assessed to pay a contribution. In the ten years between 1981/82 and 1991/92, the percentage of certificates where the assisted person was assessed for no contribution rose from 76.5 to 83.9 per cent. This reveals a pattern in which civil legal aid is becoming increasingly the province of those in receipt of the lowest levels of income, rather than of those who are just that much better off.

Lord Mackay suggested in a BBC 'Panorama' programme that any decline in eligibility might reflect rising living standards.[25] Consideration of the income limits by reference to state benefits makes this unlikely. In 1979, the lower income limit in civil cases was raised to 50 per cent above the long-term supplementary benefit rate. For 1992/93, the civil lower income limit was £3,060 per annum, less than the equivalent of £3,076 per annum received by a single pensioner on income support from October 1992. The 1992/93 legal aid allowance for a dependant under the age of 11 was £948, only 25 per cent above the income support addition of £756.60 for such a person.

The fall in eligibility has resulted from a combination of the deliberate cuts to dependants' additions in 1986 and the sporadic failure to uprate all allowances. It has particularly affected adults with child dependants: while eligibility for single pensioners fell between 1979 and 1989 from 98.2 per cent to 89.2 per cent, for a couple with two dependent children it plummeted from 75.1 per cent to a bare 33.8 per cent. These figures have been calculated by a statistician at the London School of Economics, Michael Murphy, using government figures on income from the Family Expenditure Survey. (His paper on legal aid eligibility in Great Britain between 1979 and 1990 is included in appendix 1.)

The Lord Chancellor's Department produced its rival statistics in June 1991. These indicate little change – a fall from 73.8 per cent of the population eligible in 1979 to 66.1 per cent in 1990 (69.2 per cent in personal injury cases).[26] To obtain this result, the Lord Chancellor's Department included the effect of a change of rules introduced in April 1990 allowing children to apply for legal aid on the basis of their own income and capital, not that of their parents. This is legitimate in relation, for instance, to personal injury cases, but most potentially legal aided cases concern adults – some, such as matters arising from divorce, exclusively so.

The discrepancy is also due to the Lord Chancellor's Department's less sophisticated use of data. Civil legal aid eligibility is crucially affected by housing costs, which are an allowable expense for a legal aid applicant. A high estimate of housing costs gives a high level of eligibility for groups of the population with incomes of a particular level. The important difference in methodology is that the Lord Chancellor's Department assumes average housing costs of about £100 per week as against Michael Murphy's figure which is around £30 lower. The latter is more in line with actual housing costs identified in other government figures (specifically the Housing and Construction Statistics 1979/89) for people paying mortgages and council rents. Almost all couples with two children are in one of these two categories, suggesting that Michael Murphy's figures can be relied upon, particularly for the group most affected by the decline in eligibility.[27]

A further problem is that relative eligibility levels are inconsistent.

Green form eligibility for a couple with two dependent children has, for instance, plummeted from 57.2 per cent of the population in that category to 22.5 per cent – significantly below both that of the average for the population as a whole (39.2 per cent) and their own eligibility level for civil legal aid (33.8 per cent). This imbalance may be the result of historical accident, rather than any deliberate intention. However, it exists, and hard-pressed families with young children suffer the consequences of the lack of co-ordination between the different legal aid schemes.

Government pronouncements on the purpose of civil legal aid have, in any case, changed markedly, reflecting less commitment to the scheme. In 1949, the Lord Chancellor's Department confidently asserted the purpose of legal aid to be that 'No one will be financially unable to prosecute a just and reasonable claim or defend a legal right.' By the time of its 1991 eligibility review, its tone had changed: legal aid had become 'a conditional financial support, provided by the taxpayer, for individuals whose financial circumstances would prevent them from taking or defending proceedings without assistance with their costs'.[28]

Public awareness

In order to use services, people must know about them. Public awareness of CABx is high – one poll put it at 90 per cent. Knowledge of the legal aid scheme is much lower. In 1990, only 45 per cent of those asked by Gallup to name any scheme which provided help with solicitors' costs mentioned legal aid, and seven out of ten people said that they did not understand the legal aid scheme. Most people who do know about legal aid see it as providing help with criminal charges or matrimonial problems. Few regard it as a general scheme: in the Gallup survey, only 16 per cent mentioned it as helping with housing matters, and only 3 per cent with debt. Other statistics suggest that a similarly low level of awareness exists even among those who have attempted to seek help with a problem.[29]

The Rushcliffe report stressed that the legal aid scheme 'should be given proper publicity at all times'. However, the scheme has been advertised on national TV only once – in 1973, before the launch of the green form scheme. Research indicated a dramatic short-term impact: knowledge of the scheme was raised from around one-quarter to almost half of the population. But, a year later, the figure had slipped back to 27 per cent. In addition, the advertising was more successful in reaching the middle classes than the poor.[30]

The legal aid advisory committee commented: 'Experience has taught us that mass publicity for the legal aid scheme, beyond the minimum necessary to explain the scheme to users by leaflets etc, is not good value for money'. It was argued that too much would be spent in reaching people not likely to use legal aid. Instead, it recommended a more selective approach, directed at 'advisory workers' in contact with those having legal problems.[31]

Since then, the Law Society and Legal Aid Board have experimented with various methods of publicity, including a video in post office queues. Leaflets and forms have been improved, with 'Crystal Mark' recognition by the Plain English Campaign for the most recent non-matrimonial civil legal aid form. There has also been more translation into minority languages. However, in a 1992 report, the National Audit Office found that 'awareness of legal aid is low, even among the eligible population'. It considered that 'The Board's publicity is informative and explanatory rather than advertising and is more likely to be used by those who have already identified a need for legal services.' Furthermore, it added: 'There is a lack of accurate information about specialist services offered by practitioners, for example in such matters as social security, housing and debt.'[32]

The Legal Aid Board, in the same way as the Law Society before it, has not been effective in ensuring general knowledge of the legal aid scheme. To a limited extent, this has been counterbalanced by the initiative of individual solicitors who have undertaken advertising campaigns – one firm in Liverpool has even paid for radio advertisements on an issue as specific as compensation for one particular industrial disease, vibration white finger. The North Western Legal Services Committee also launched an advertising campaign for personal injury litigation which was then taken up nationally by the Law Society.

Lack of knowledge remains, however, a feature in depressing demand for services, particularly outside criminal and matrimonial work. In Part III we discuss how the question of education and information is approached in other jurisdictions; in this country, no institution – be it a government department, the Legal Aid Board or the Law Society – has ever accepted overall responsibility for the production of information (for instance, a guide to divorce law) on the workings of English law.

Quality, cost and remuneration

Lord Mackay, in his letter setting out the aims and objectives for the newly established Legal Aid Board in July 1988, required it to review 'existing targets and indicators for performance' in relation not only to legal aid administration but also to legal aid practice itself.[33] This has encouraged the board to look at the quality of work undertaken by legal aid practitioners in a way that would have probably been impossible for the Law Society.

Control of quality has become a major concern for the Legal Aid Board. From the beginning, it has identified contracts as 'franchises' with service providers as a key means of achieving this aim. 'Franchising', it stated in an early consultation document, 'involves identifying those who can satisfy criteria of competence and reliability, assisting and encouraging them by freeing them from some of the restrictions now applying to legal aid.'[34] Its approach was initially influenced by the techniques of 'total quality management'. In consequence, its franchising specification seeks to detail all the indicators of quality, such as books and training, that should lead to high quality service provision. The problem is that indicators of quality are not necessarily determinants of it. A practitioner with a wonderful library at his or her disposal may still conduct cases badly or choose to cut corners in order to maximise profits.

The board is now developing the concept of the monitoring of 'transaction criteria'. It describes these as 'a series of points and questions that a trained observer checking a file after the event would use to evaluate what was done and the standard to which it was done'.[35] The academic researchers working on the concept for the board have explained that they are seeking to identify a 'competence threshold' which fits modern management thinking on quality – 'not perfection but "fitness for purpose"'. They raise a potential conflict with the board's involvement in this issue: 'the purposive definition of quality leaves it open to funders of a service in times of budgetary constraint to redefine its purpose so that it requires a low level of performance. All this, of course, underlines the importance of determining *who* is to define the appropriate level of service to be delivered' (see p146).

The Law Society believes that quality is simply a reflection of price. One of its arguments against any extension of legal aid payments by fixed fees, as opposed to hourly rates, is that quality will suffer. The Society recently launched a well-publicised campaign on this issue – some local law societies even associated themselves with the withdrawal of their members from police station and court duty solicitor schemes in protest at the low remuneration rates for magistrates' court representation proposed by the Lord Chancellor.

Quality, remuneration and cost, then, dominate much contemporary debate about the state of legal aid and publicly funded legal services. As this chapter has shown, other issues are also important to those seeking to use those services. These include lack of provision in relation to social welfare law, the effects of a divided profession and divided provision, the lack of an overall strategy for publicly funded legal services as a whole, declining civil legal aid eligibility and lack of information about legal aid and legal services. The chapters in Part II consider four specific areas of work in order to analyse whether other issues emerge which need to be addressed in any reform.

References

1　Speech, 4 October 1991.
2　*The Government's Expenditure Plans 1991–92 to 1993–94: The Lord Chancellor's and Law Officers' Departments* Cm 1510, HMSO, 1991, p1.
3　Legal Aid Board *Annual Report 1991–92* HC 50, HMSO, 1992, from which all figures in this chapter for 1991/92 are taken unless otherwise indicated. Crown Court figures from *HC Answers* 1 July 1992, col 575.
4　*Legal Aid Efficiency Scrutiny: the Law Society's Response* Law Society, 1976, para I.5.
5　*Annual Statistical Report 1991* Law Society, 1991, p31.
6　Bar Council's Strategy Group *Strategies for the Future* The General Council of the Bar, 1990, figure 4, p18.
7　As in 5, p31.
8　As in 5, p33.
9　*Survey of Legal Aid Provision* Law Society, 1988.
10　J Baldwin and S Hill *The Operation of the Green Form Scheme in England and Wales* Lord Chancellor's Department, 1988, p23.
11　Civil Justice Review *Housing Cases* Lord Chancellor's Department, 1987, para 81.
12　D Forbes and S Wright *Housing Cases in Nine CABx* unpublished, 1990.
13　H Genn and Y Genn *The Effectiveness of Representation at Tribunals* Lord Chancellor's Department, 1989, p24.
14　As in 13, p70.
15　M Blacksell, K Economides, C Watkins *Access to Justice in Rural Britain: project working paper 6* University of Exeter, 1988, p35.
16　As in 6.
17　Amendment inserted into Rule 502(b) *Code of Conduct of the Bar of England and Wales* General Council of the Bar, 1990.
18　The Lord Chancellor's Advisory Committee on Legal Education and

Conduct *Advice to the Law Society on its application for authorisation to grant extended rights of audience to solicitors* LCAC, 1992.

19 The National Association of Citizens Advice Bureaux *Annual Report 1990/ 91* p18.

20 Legal Aid Efficiency Scrutiny *Report, Volume 1* Lord Chancellor's Department, 1986, para 4.7.

21 As in 3 above, p23.

22 As in 19 above, p18 and p5.

23 As in 19 above, p4.

24 *HL Hansard debates* 18 March 1986, col 921.

25 BBC Panorama interview with J Rozenberg, 17 April 1989.

26 Review of Financial Conditions for Legal Aid *Eligibility for Civil Legal Aid: a consultation paper* Lord Chancellor's Department, 1991, p85.

27 M Murphy *An analysis of the differences in eligibility for civil legal aid in 1989* unpublished, copies available from LAG, price £2.

28 Lord Chancellor *Summary of the Proposed New Service* Cmnd 7563, 1948, and Review of Financial Conditions for Legal Aid Eligibility, as in 26 above, para 1.

29 Broadcasting Research Department *Citizens Advice Bureaux: the price of advice* BBC, 1986, and Social Surveys (Gallup Poll) Ltd *Legal Aid Publicity* unpublished, 1990.

30 Schlackman Research Organisation *An investigation into current awareness and knowledge of the Legal Advice and Assistance scheme among recommenders and potential clients* April 1975.

31 *27th Legal Aid Annual Reports* [1976–77] HC 172, HMSO, p82.

32 National Audit Office *The Administration of Legal Aid in England and Wales* HC 90, HMSO, 1992, p31.

33 Legal Aid Board *Report to the Lord Chancellor* Cm 688, HMSO, 1989, p24.

34 *Second Stage Consultation on the Future of the Green Form Scheme* Legal Aid Board, 1989, para 21.

35 As in 3, p24.

36 A Paterson and A Sherr, 'Quality, Clients and Legal Aid' *New Law Journal* 5 June 1992, p783.

Part II

Studies in legal needs

CHAPTER 3

Family disputes

A key impetus in the development of the legal aid scheme after the second world war was the need for publicly funded divorce litigation (see chapter 1). Today, matrimonial cases remain the largest single area of civil legal aid work: in 1991/92, the net cost of legal aid and advice in matrimonial and family proceedings was £192 million, accounting for nearly one-fifth of all legal aid expenditure.[1] This chapter, by providing a picture of the involvement of legal aid and legally aided practitioners in one particular field of legal work, indicates the integral link between legal aid, legal procedure and legal reform.

In 1989, the divorce rate in the United Kingdom was over 12 per 1,000 marriages, one of the highest in Europe; 151,000 divorces were granted in England and Wales in that year.[2] The following statistics indicate the scale of current matrimonial work. Notably, although the number of matrimonial and family cases has grown over the last decade, these take up a decreasing proportion of civil legal aid certificates.

	1991/92	1981/82[3]
Green form (bills paid)		
Matrimonial	231,065	182,898
Family	204,584	139,642
Percentage of all green forms	35	49
ABWOR (bills paid)		
Family, children, etc	62,182	57,291
Percentage of total	94	100
Civil legal aid (certificates issued)		
Matrimonial	146,437	104,403
Percentage of total	43	67

A significant proportion of legal aided matrimonial and family work involves emergency situations. About 13 per cent of all full legal aid certificates were preceded by an emergency certificate; 16,819 certificates related expressly to domestic violence, and another 34,634 covered an application for some form of injunction.

Legal aid is only rarely granted for divorce itself – in 1991/92 defended divorces accounted for only 2,188 certificates. The vast majority of certificates related to matrimonial 'ancillary relief' – concerning maintenance, division of assets and children. In addition, 16,106 of the 190,864 certificates classified as 'non-matrimonial' related to other matters concerning children, such as adoption, guardianship and child abduction.

An undoubted difference between matrimonial and non-matrimonial legal aid is the impact of the statutory charge. In matrimonial cases, it is particularly rare for legally aided clients to recover their full costs from the other side: in 1991/92, the legal aid fund recovered only £3.7 million in this way (compared with £91.9 million in non-matrimonial civil cases).[4] The net cost of matrimonial legal aid is, however, considerably reduced by the effect of the statutory charge. Maintenance payments and the first £2,500 of lump-sum payments are exempt (the latter limit was set in 1976 and has not since been amended). But the Legal Aid Board can claw back costs from any property 'recovered or preserved in the proceedings', and although litigants may lack income resources, occupation and ownership of the former matrimonial home is often settled in the proceedings. The statutory charge operates on property in the same way as a mortgage (charges registered since 1989 carry interest at 12 per cent). When a house is sold, clients are normally required to repay the capital, though the board will sometimes allow the charge to be transferred to a new home.

In 1991/92, the effect of the statutory charge meant that £27.9 million, representing 7.9 per cent of the total awarded or agreed, was retained, arising from 17,249 cases. The importance of the charge in matrimonial cases can be seen by comparing this with the amount retained in non-matrimonial cases: just £6.8 million, representing 2.2 per cent, from 4,557 cases.[5]

Legal aid costs in matrimonial cases show evidence of the inflationary trend that so concerns the government and the Legal Aid Board. Board statistics reveal that the price of an average High Court matrimonial case rose from £989 in 1981/82 to £2,537 in 1991/92 (£1,438 at 1981/82 prices) representing a rise in real terms of 45 per cent. The equivalent figures for a county court action show a rise in real terms of 83 per cent.

But these price rises are not necessarily attributable to unreasonable cost increases by lawyers; it is also possible that matrimonial cases have grown more difficult over the last decade. One obvious factor is the growth in house ownership: the percentage of owner-occupied dwellings rose from 55 per cent in 1980 to over two-thirds in 1991.[6] Another is that occupational pension rights now feature more in disputes on the breakdown of a marriage. A third factor is that acceptance of traditional roles may be changing: women are clearly increasingly unwilling to tolerate domestic violence; men may possibly be more inclined to demand greater contact with their children.

Quality of service

The quality of solicitors' work in matrimonial cases has been the subject of three specific criticisms: first, that solicitors are orientated towards confrontation rather than consensus; second, that they give insufficient information about costs; third, that they have an inadequate knowledge of how the welfare benefits system interacts with financial settlements in divorce.

A bias towards confrontation is not surprising: clients consult solicitors precisely because they want to deal with a conflict. A professional tendency to take action rather than listen to people's problems is also encouraged by the system of legal aid remuneration, which pays higher rates for litigation than for advice and assistance. Some solicitors have, however, developed considerable conciliation skills, to the benefit of their clients. The increasing involvement of solicitors in mediation schemes indicates a willingness to move towards resolving disputes outside a court situation. One commentator has even suggested that counselling offered by lawyers is often preferred by clients, because talking to lawyers, rather than social workers or probation officers, is seen as free from stigma: 'an approach for legal service, while valid in its own terms, may also act as a face-saving mechanism, allowing people to receive covert emotional support without loss of self-respect'.[7] Changes introduced by the Children Act 1990, whereby a divorcing couple must seek agreement on arrangements for children before issuing proceedings, may encourage a shift towards more pre-proceedings conciliation – as would implementation of the Law Commission's proposals for changing divorce procedure considered below (see p38).

The second criticism – that solicitors do not give clients enough information about their fees – is not limited to matrimonial work.

However, the high impact of the statutory charge in this area means that clients end up paying for much of their representation; legal aid operates merely as a loan. If clients are to be expected to meet their costs, they must know what their bill is likely to be and must be given some control over how it is run up. A long-standing complaint, that solicitors often failed to inform their clients of the statutory charge,[8] has been remedied – solicitors must now give clients a leaflet explaining its existence. But this is not enough. The Law Society's professional written standards giving guidance on 'good practice' states that privately paying clients should be informed that they can put a limit on how far costs may be incurred before the lawyer makes further reference to them. Legally aided clients are, however, excluded from this provision.[9] So, although they often end up paying for the service they receive, they can exercise less influence over the cost of their litigation than a private client.

Solicitors are criticised in another area which can crucially affect a client's financial situation: their advice, or rather lack of it, on welfare benefits. A recent study of the welfare benefits work in ten Liverpool firms concluded that: 'generally the possibility of entitlement to or increase in benefit was only rarely brought to the client's attention by the adviser . . . If the quality of matrimonial work is to be judged partly on the extent to which all financial aspects of matrimonial breakdown and divorce are covered, there was a clear deficiency among several of the survey firms.'[10] An ignorance of the benefits system is, to some extent, understandable, as the field is not well covered in solicitors' professional training. But, whatever the reason, some way must be found to improve the quality of this aspect of the service. This could be done if the Legal Aid Board imposed contractual terms as to the basis on which it will fund services – a process which has begun with the franchising experiment. Alternatively, or additionally, the Law Society could take responsibility for increasing its members' knowledge through better initial training or some form of specialisation scheme. The desirable relationship between these two approaches is discussed further in chapter 14 (see p146).

Integrating legal reform

An issue that arises in considering publicly funded legal services in matrimonial cases is the link between delivery of legal services and reforms in law and procedure. This is illustrated by the reforms announced in 1976 by the then Lord Chancellor, Lord Elwyn Jones, which stand as the clearest example of an integrated approach to the reform of legal aid and legal provision.[11]

Lord Elwyn Jones' proposal was that divorce procedure should be changed so that undefended hearings ceased to require a hearing in open court; legal aid could, thereby, be withdrawn. Civil legal aid would, henceforth, be available only for ancillary applications relating to children and financial matters. In divorce cases not involving such ancillary matters, only green form legal advice would be available. The savings from this move, which should become apparent after two years, could then be used to lift eligibility levels, to fund further law centres in areas of need and to cut the overall cost of legal aid.

The Law Society reacted to the proposal with hostility. The *Law Society's Gazette* called the proposals 'a body blow for legal aid' and warned that the hardest hit sector of the profession would be firms 'providing a service in the poorer areas of our cities'.[12] The Society, it continued, had 'a good deal of evidence that solicitors are finding it impossible in some areas to do legal aid work at all because of the failure of legal aid costs to keep pace with the rise in overheads'. Nevertheless, the divorce reforms were enacted, and financial eligibility limits were increased just before the 1979 election. Although, with the fall of the Labour government, the law centres never received their extra funding, this planned shift of resources represents a model of how legal aid reform must be approached.

The 1976 reforms represented a move away from formal court judgment to an alternative type of dispute resolution, whereby divorce was largely dealt with as a paper transaction and ancillary matters in a less formal hearing. A number of other suggestions for change have been made involving a shift to conciliation, or mediation. These have been seen as offering a way of removing lawyers from matrimonial disputes, encouraging settlements and furthering a move to alternative dispute resolution outside the courts.

The notion of conciliation in matrimonial cases was first put on the political agenda by the Finer Committee Report on One-Parent Families in 1974. It made a careful distinction between 'reconciliation' (that is, reuniting spouses) and 'conciliation', defined as 'assisting the parties to deal with the consequences of the established breakdown of their marriage, whether resulting in divorce or separation, by reaching agreements or giving consents or reducing the area of conflict'.[13] Such a definition can, and indeed does, cover a great variety of approaches and schools of thought.

The Finer committee proposed that conciliation should cover all post-divorce arrangements, including financial support. In practice, however, conciliation (now more generally known as mediation) has concentrated on matters relating to what used, before the Children Act 1990, to be known as access and custody disputes. Conciliation has developed largely as an addition to court procedures, not as an alternative. This was probably unavoidable since matters relating to children had, until recently, ultimately to be considered at a judicial hearing.

Finer's judgment was that conciliation schemes, even operating at the last moment during the course of a divorce, 'have substantial success in civilising the consequences of the breakdown [of the relationship between the parties]'.[14] A more recent study commissioned by the Lord Chancellor's Department came to the same conclusion: 'conciliation [except court-based schemes with high judicial control] is at least as effective as other, more traditional procedures in generating satisfactory settlements and on several measures of effectiveness often achieves much more than that. In terms of psychological well-being, independent services scored particularly well.'[15]

The development of conciliation services has floundered because of the costs. The study referred to above estimated in 1989 that a national court-based conciliation service might be provided for around £1.9m and an independent service for about £3.3m.[16] It concluded, 'whether a national conciliation service should be established is a matter for political judgment since conciliation involves positive resource costs'.[17]

The Law Commission avoided expressing an opinion on conciliation when, in 1988, it gave its view on how divorce law might be reformed. It argued for what it called a 'process system', requiring all matters relating to the irretrievable breakdown of a relationship to be determined before a divorce decree could be granted. The commission's support for conciliation was, however, clear: 'Divorce is for most people a difficult and painful process during which they may well need professional help and support. Whether [a conciliation service] should be made available is not a matter for law reform . . . The . . . procedure which we describe below should give both the opportunity and incentive for such conciliation to take place but we do not suggest that it be made a mandatory requirement.'[18]

Current legal aid rules do not encourage the use of independent mediation services. Neither green form nor civil legal aid can be used to cover mediation itself, though an allowance of £32.50 (including solicitors' costs of £9.50) is payable for the kind of report that might be the outcome of a mediation process. The Family Mediators Association, however, estimates that the average cost of its standard mediation, covering about five hours, is £300 per party.[19]

Another reform stalled on cost considerations is the development of a family court which would unite the existing jurisdictions of the High, county and magistrates' court. First put forward by the Finer committee, the proposal has gained considerable support since, but successive governments have moved only very cautiously in the direction of a unified family court. The reason is evident in the comparison between the average cost of a legal aid matrimonial case of only £335 in the magistrates' court as compared with £1,432 in the county court in 1991/92.

Magistrates' courts are unsuitable for family cases because of their association with crime. Moreover, they have tended to be used by poorer clients, whereas those with higher incomes use the better equipped county and High courts. This form of social apartheid may well now be being mitigated to some extent by the recently enlarged role of the county courts and the increasing use of the magistrates' courts for enforcing orders rather than for making them. The situation remains, however, unsatisfactory.

By contrast, reform of child support legislation has raced ahead. The Child Support Agency will soon begin taking responsibility for the determination, through a set formula, of maintenance for children and its collection. Such cases will be removed from the courts and the limited appeal rights that have been retained will be excercised within the Independent Tribunal Service (formerly the social security appeals tribunals). *Children Come First*, the white paper heralding the legislation that established the agency, gave detailed costing of the savings for the Department of Social Security involved in this reform. It found that 'the direct administrative costs of the present maintenance system [presumably in 1989/90] are £50.8 million per annum', with the DSS costing £30.7 million, the magistrates' courts £13.7 million, and the High Court and county court £6.2 million.[20] It concluded that substantial savings could be made by replacing the arrangements whereby parents, generally mothers, or the DSS, sued for maintenance. Under the new system, the Child Support Agency will operate on a purely administrative basis. No appeal will be possible as to an assessment of maintenance due; only liability will be contestable.

The Lord Chancellor, who co-sponsored this legislation, was unable to give any figures for the projected savings to legal aid – reflecting a wider failure to ensure that adequate information on legal aid expenditure is kept. The statistics in the white paper showed that, in 1989/90, £73.5

million was spent on ancillary relief in the High Court and county court, and a further £5.1 million on magistrates' court orders.[21] But no distinction was made between the costs of maintenance and property orders in the higher courts – the proportion spent on child maintenance was just said to be 'modest'. Equally, the Lord Chancellor's Department failed to consider other needs and consequences of such a major reform. For example, when similar child support legislation was introduced in Australia, the need for information and education was recognised: the legal aid commissions in each state were involved in a range of initiatives, including running classes for women to help them understand and deal with their equivalent of the Child Support Agency.

The government has too easily assumed that women will automatically benefit from the introduction of such legislation in this country. This will not necessarily be the case – as evidence from Australia makes clear: in some instances, the Australian agency has proved slow to obtain maintenance and, on occasions, it has made mistakes over liability. In addition, the formula to be administered by the Child Support Agency for calculating maintenance will tend to shift resources from the second families of many men to their first families. This may lead to other problems, with implications for legal aid. None of this appears to have been considered by the Lord Chancellor's Department or the Legal Aid Board.

The trend away from judicial determination of family matters, in favour of their resolution through negotiation and conciliation, reveals how important it is that policy-makers also consider the use of publicly funded legal services. Such a shift is not necessarily less expensive – indeed, an adequate system of mediation, backed by access to the courts where necessary, may cost significantly more than current arrangements

Further reforms of matrimonial law seems imminent, with the government clearly attracted to implementation of the Law Commission proposals referred to earlier. This short study of family disputes shows that it is possible to shift resources spent on legal services, as was successfully done with the 1976 reforms. However, all possible consequences of any reform must be considered, necessitating the involvement in policy-making of the Legal Aid Board, with its practical experience of expenditure patterns, and legal aid practitioners and advisers, with their knowledge of clients' needs. Furthermore, the hope of achieving financial savings while, at the same time, improving services for those involved in the breakdown of their personal relationships may prove naive.

References

1 Legal Aid Board *Annual Report 1991–92* HC 50, HMS0, 1992, p1.
2 Central Statistical Office *Social Trends 22* HMSO, 1992, table 2.16, p45.
3 As in 1 above, and *32nd Legal Aid Annual Reports [1981–82]* HC 189, HMSO, 1982.
4 As in 1 above, p 87.
5 As in 1 above, p60.
6 Central Statistical Office *Social Trends 12* HMSO, 1982, p146, as in 2 above, p45, and as in 1 above, p59.
7 M Murch *Justice and Welfare in Divorce* Sweet and Maxwell, 1980, p35.
8 Eg, G Davis and K Bader, 'Client Costs: a failure to inform', February 1985 *Legal Action* 7–9.
9 *The Guide to Professional Conduct of Solicitors 1990* Law Society, 1990, p63, para 3(c).
10 N Harris 'Judging the quality of welfare benefits work by firms of solicitors' (1991) *Civil Justice Quaterly* pp311, 325–6.
11 *HL Hansard debates* 15 July 1976, cols 1212–1220.
12 *Law Society's Gazette* 23 June 1976.
13 *Report of the Committee on One-parent Families* Volume 1, Cmnd 5629, HMSO, 1974, para 4.288.
14 As in 13, para 4.312.
15 Conciliation Project Unit *Report to the Lord Chancellor on the costs and effectiveness of conciliation in England and Wales* University of Newcastle on Tyne, 1989, para 20.11.
16 As in 15, para 20.13f.
17 As in 15, para 20.48.
18 Law Commission *Facing the Future: a discussion paper on the ground for divorce* HC 479, HMSO, 1988, para 5.33.
19 L Parkinson *The need for publicly funded family mediation services: legal aid implications* Family Mediators Association, 1992.
20 *Children Come First* Volume 2, Cm 1263, HMSO, 1990, para 6.1.
21 As in 20, para 6.21.

CHAPTER 4

Personal injury

Personal injury not only represents the second largest category of case for which civil legal aid is granted, but also an area where a considerable amount of litigation is conducted without legal aid. After conveyancing, crime and family breakdown, a personal injury is the most common eventuality that brings ordinary people into contact with the legal system.

Personal injury work is, in consequence, important for a large section of the legal profession. Litigation in this area is the staple fare of many barristers, and most high street solicitors handle some personal injury work from time to time. However, increasingly, personal injury is becoming an area for specialisation. Some large and prosperous firms are beginning to establish a near-monopoly in multi-party litigation involving disasters or product liability actions.

A large amount of reliable data exists in relation to personal injury. The Pearson Commission on Liability for Personal Injuries investigated the subject after the legal process had shown itself unable, for a multiplicity of reasons, to provide compensation for the victims of the Thalidomide tragedy.[1] The commission reported in 1978 and, although its recommendations were largely unimplemented, it built up a body of empirical research which is still useful. The subject has also been well researched elsewhere.

There has been no shortage of ideas for reform. Besides Pearson, which recommended a move towards a 'no-fault' system of compensation, there have been a number of proposals for change. Most recently, multi-party litigation has been the subject of inquiry by the Legal Aid Board, which has now published new procedures on how it will deal with such cases.[2] The Civil Justice Review recommended that the Lord Chancellor should consider 'the feasibility of a no-fault scheme, restricted to less serious road accidents and financed by private insurance'.[3] The medical profession backed a private member's bill proposing a no-fault compensation scheme to replace the present system of medical malpractice liability.[4] The government issued a green paper on contingency fees, whereby lawyers' costs are paid only if their client is successful. These are particularly relevant to personal injury cases because they involve money damages and costs.[5] The Law Society has raised the question of whether a contingency legal aid fund should be established along the lines of that in Hong Kong and some Australian states.[6]

Despite all this interest, personal injury litigation continues to give rise to concern. Victims of disasters and major drug failures still fail to obtain compensation, while Pearson's suggestion for a comprehensive reshaping of the system to allow a greater role for the state was ignored. What reform has been introduced has been of a piecemeal nature. For instance, a large number of personal injury cases have been transferred from the High Court to the county court – with very mixed consequences in terms of the courts' ability to cope.

The extent of need

In 1978, the Pearson commission estimated that every year around 3 million people in the UK were injured sufficiently seriously to have their normal activities interrupted for at least four days, and claimed that 'no more than 3 per cent of men and 8 per cent of women will escape [such] injury. . . during an average lifetime'.[7] About two-thirds of those injured each year blamed someone else for their injuries or might be in a position to consider suing for compensation.

The number of legal aid certificates for personal injury cases has risen in recent years, as the following table indicates:[8]

Type of case	1986/87	1991/92
Road accidents	16,281	19,637
Accidents at work	9,648	19,047
Medical negligence	4,547	18,666
Other personal injury	n/a	24,757

his shows that there has been a fourfold increase in medical negligence cases and that certificates for accidents at work have doubled. Over the same period, the total number of non-matrimonial certificates rose from 118,780 to 190,864, an increase of only 60 per cent. Despite the increase in the use of legal aid, a substantial amount of legal assistance is available from other sources. Unions assist at least 90,000 members a year with legal cases, of which the TUC estimates that 88 per cent relate to accidents at work. Around 34,000 enquiries a year are made to the AA's claims recovery service in respect of road accidents.[9]

The reasons for this increase in litigation are unclear. Partly, there may be greater consumer awareness: claimants tell their friends and relatives; some of the higher awards are reported in the press, and word spreads. Partly, there may be less faith that the national health service and social security system will provide for an injured person's needs. In addition, there is a growing emphasis on citizens' rights. In the case of accidents, this may encourage suing those who are felt to be to blame. There is also a demand for greater accountability, reflected in attempts to secure prosecutions for corporate manslaughter in serious accident cases. People also seem more prepared to challenge professionals such as doctors or teachers. Even so, the increase has been from a very small base: it is still the case that only a small minority – probably no more than 10 per cent – of those injured other than on the roads or at work make a claim.

The role of solicitors

In order to claim, injured parties need to know their rights and how to set about enforcing them. Studies show that those injured on the roads or at work are much more likely to claim than those injured elsewhere. In addition, employed people are more likely to see solicitors than others.[10] This may be attributable partly to widespread knowledge of the existence of compulsory insurance for drivers and employers. It may also be due to the prevailing standard of legal liability, which makes it difficult for some (for example, people injured in the home) to prove that another party has been at fault.

A small minority of claimants – again under 10 per cent – try to claim compensation themselves. The evidence suggests that they do not do well. They tend to be fobbed off with tiny offers – much less than a solicitor would advise them to accept. Realistically, the first step to a successful claim is to see a solicitor, but only a minority of potential claimants gets as far as a solicitor's office.

People can only seek advice on a personal injury claim if they have some way of meeting the cost of that advice. Those sponsored by a trade union, which will pay its own legal bill and, if necessary, that of the other side without deductions or contributions, are in the strongest position. Trade unions deal with many cases in-house; they place others with a limited number of specialist solicitors known to provide an expert service with whom they have developed a relationship. Trade unions are also an important source of knowledge about the alternative, statutory scheme for industrial injuries compensation.

Legal aid is not always drawn upon, even in cases where it is available. Put off by the low pay and administrative hassle involved with legal aid, many solicitors routinely omit to fulfil their professional obligation to advise clients of their right to legal aid. Instead, if a case seems straightforward, the solicitor may suggest going ahead on the basis that the costs will be paid by the other side once a settlement is reached. Known in Scotland as acting 'speculatively' or 'on spec', this is a form of contingency fee to be made lawful by the Courts and Legal Services Act 1990. For the solicitor, it has the advantage of not having to deal with the legal aid authorities; but there may be disadvantages for the client. Insurers take legally aided claims much more seriously and make higher offers, because they know that plaintiffs can go to court if they need to. Clients on legal aid are also protected against paying costs if they later lose or abandon their claim.[11]

For those who do not qualify for legal aid, are not in trade unions and are not covered by legal expenses insurance (which covers around 7 per cent of the population[12]), speculative arrangements are usually the only option. But solicitors will generally limit themselves to cases which they are sure can be won. They are unlikely to take a medical accident or defective drug case on such a basis, because of the large initial outlay and the uncertainties of success. A few clients will use their own money, but the potential risks are high.

A survey of accident compensation conducted by the Oxford Centre for Socio-Legal Research in 1984 found that just under three-quarters of those consulting a solicitor received some money, nearly always as a result of an out-of-court settlement. The rest decided either not to make a claim or, having started one, to abandon it.[13] The Legal Aid Board's figures tell a similar story. Of cases closed in 1990/91, 83 per cent of those for road accidents, 78 per cent of those for work accidents and 68 per cent of other personal injury cases resulted in court victory or favourable settlement.[14] But in medical negligence cases, only 42 per cent of plaintiffs received a payment. Many such cases are so complex that it takes expert investigation to tell whether or not there is a potential claim. The board usually issues authority to take certain initial steps on a case and legal aid is withdrawn if good grounds are not established.

The main charges levelled at the compensation process are that it takes too long, costs too much, subjects claimants to too much uncertainty and provides them with inadequate compensation. The Oxford study, which described the course of a personal injury action as an 'obstacle race', found that over half of all cases took 16 months to settle. As for those in which court proceedings are started, they take even longer, and the process is costly.[15] In 1985, the Civil Justice Review found that where London High Court actions were begun, the parties' bills averaged £6,830.[16]

Difficulties of proof lead to the abandoning of some cases. A further disincentive is provided by the uncertain nature of the sum to be awarded at the end of a case. This is calculated according to complex and unpredictable rules and may be subject to deductions for contributory negligence. Another problem is created by the effect of a defendant paying a sum in damages into court. If the plaintiffs continue their action and recover less, they lose their indemnity for costs and end up paying legal costs out of their damages. Because of these factors, non-specialist solicitors tend to take a conciliatory approach and may allow a case to drag on until negotiations finally break down, by which time vital evidence may have disappeared. There is also evidence that non-specialists find it difficult to establish efficient case-preparation systems or to keep up to date with court procedure.[17] If defendants realise that a plaintiff's solicitor is unlikely to press the matter in court, they will offer less.

Thus, negotiated settlements are both common and crucial in personal injury cases. Yet the fact that most plaintiffs must rely on their solicitor's advice when it comes to deciding whether to accept an offer, raises a possible conflict of interest. Settlement normally brings full and immediate payment of costs, whereas, if a case goes to court, errors in preparation may be exposed, payment of costs will be delayed, and items disallowed on taxation. There is an obvious pressure to agree to settlements which, at present, are subject to no outside evaluation. The Lord Chancellor is considering a scheme whereby the Legal Aid Board will monitor settlements against the amount solicitors predict at the start of the case. This, however, could create an incentive to make low predictions and recommend low settlements. There has been an urgent need for the Law Society to take a lead in improving standards. Its proposed specialist personal injury panel may contribute to this.

Multi-party claims

Multi-party litigation – cases in which numerous plaintiffs sue together in respect of the same cause of action – gives rise to special difficulties for the legal system. Some of the problems, which arise primarily from court procedures, are outside the scope of this book. Others, relating to funding and the relationship between clients and their solicitors, reveal weaknesses in the legal aid scheme.

The Opren case – in which 1,500 people alleged that they had been injured by an anti-arthritis drug, and sued both the manufacturers and the government department which had licensed the drug – cruelly exposed a number of problems with legal aid. Around two-thirds were legally aided; of those above the means test, most were elderly people with savings to supplement their pensions. In 1987, the plaintiffs' lawyers selected a few legally aided, representative 'lead' cases for trial which would determine the outcome for the whole group. It was hoped that in this way the legal aid fund would bear the costs and the risks of the trial. Instead, the trial judge ordered that the costs of the action should be shared equally between all the plaintiffs. Thus, if the action failed, each plaintiff without legal aid would be responsible for paying their proportion of the total plaintiffs' and defendants' bill – a suggested £6 million. Few plaintiffs could afford to risk their life savings on such a venture, and many were on the point of withdrawing when a millionaire benefactor stepped in to underwrite the claims – a move which allowed the case to continue and, eventually, a settlement to be reached.

In 1988, this issue was raised during the debates on the Legal Aid Bill in the House of Lords. The Lord Chancellor, acknowledging public concern, agreed that the problem should be looked at by the Legal Aid Board.[18] In due course, the board published a consultation paper recommending extension of the means test in group actions: the marginal costs of including extra people within the group, it argued, would be small; in fact, the fund would benefit from the additional contributions which those above the normal means test would bring.[19] The board's final report, however, did not recommend extended legal aid; nor did it see a case for limiting the effect of the statutory charge (see p5) in group cases, to which it is clearly unsuited.[20]

There are further difficulties for clients involved in multi-party litigation. In practice, most litigation centres on 'action groups' run by committed individuals who personally bear the costs of co-ordinating the group and issuing information. Their interests may not always coincide exactly with those of other members of the group, and there may also be friction between the group and the solicitors involved when it comes to settlements. In the Opren case, for example, most of the claims were settled, but the solicitors did not discuss the terms with the action group before agreeing them. Clients then were told that, if they did not accept the deal, their solicitors would cease to act for them. The process caused considerable disagreement and ill-feeling and the chair of the Opren Action Group later described the settlement as 'despicable and insulting'.[21] The trial judge's decision to take guarantees from the negotiating solicitors not to act for plaintiffs in any future Opren litigation – thereby limiting the client's freedom of choice – was also highly questionable.

Yet the relationship between claimants, action group and solicitors is likely to become even more complex under the Legal Aid Board's plans to contract with solicitors' firms for 'generic work' (a term connoting the preparation of the technical evidence in a case). Under these arrangements, the board alone will be able to appoint or dismiss the solicitors employed to prepare this part of a case, and will require only that claimants be kept informed. A key paragraph in the board's arrangements states: 'nothing in these arrangements shall oblige contracting firms to comply with all requests for information from local firms or claimants or to disseminate information which in the opinion of contracting firms might prejudice the interests of claimants in the action generally'.[22] Difficult conflicts of interest may arise for solicitors caught between their client and the 'generic' lawyer, who will, in effect, be acting on instructions from the Legal Aid Board. This problem has not been adequately considered.

Information

Someone who has a legal right to compensation against those who cause injuries should clearly have the opportunity to exercise that right. At present, this is not always the case. A major problem lies with access to information, a situation which could be remedied. Special efforts to encourage those in 'low-claiming' groups to come forward have been a success. In 1978, for example, the North Western Legal Services Committee distributed leaflets and posters through hospitals and advice centres, whereby accident victims could send a tear-off slip to the committee, which then arranged an interview with a solicitor free of charge. An evaluation of the scheme found that 80 per cent of those using it – many from groups which do not usually claim, such as pensioners – were advised that they had good grounds to claim.[23]

Attempts were made to launch the scheme elsewhere. At first, interest was sporadic, but, in June 1987, the Law Society relaunched it nationally under the title 'ALAS!'. It distributed half a million leaflets, produced a video for post offices and generated substantial press coverage. In the first ten months, 5,000 people used the scheme, of whom 3,000 went on to make claims.[24]

In 1990, the Law Society advertised the scheme on TV. This appeared to be a successful strategy, but the Society decided not to commit a further publicity budget to the scheme.[25] The scheme is now advertised through leaflets at CABx and on hospital appointment cards, generating between 1,000 and 1,500 enquiries a year. But a survey of solicitors participating in the scheme found that fewer than one in ten regarded it as an important source of business.[26]

The ALAS! scheme shows both the success of legal information campaigns and their limitations. Although its launch clearly had an impact, the Law Society decided not to carry on publicising it. If legal information is to be treated more seriously, it needs to be the responsibility of the body administering legal aid (see p114).

Progress

Legal aid in personal injury cases shows a certain pattern. A study undertaken by the Law Society for 1975/76 indicated that 77 per cent of all contributions paid by legally aided clients with a personal injury case were ultimately returned because costs were obtained from the defendant.[27] This led the Lord Chancellor's legal aid advisory committee to recommend that no contribution be levied in such cases and to suggest that financial eligibility might, in fact, be extended with minimal expense. In April 1990, Lord Mackay extended the income eligibility upper limit in personal injury cases above that for other categories of case.

Extending legal aid eligibility further offers more hope of increasing opportunities for those above current legal aid eligibility levels to sue. The alternative of permitting lawyers to charge contingency fees is less satisfactory. The 1988 green paper, which reported that, in the US, 'contingency fees are most used in personal injury cases where the potential award (or reward) is greatest', expressed the view that 'the main advantage of contingency fees is that they give "small" plaintiffs an opportunity of bringing their claims to court'.[28] In that context, 'small' meant those ineligible for legal aid but without sufficient resources to consider paying the full cost of litigation. But in a jurisdiction such as our own, where the potential cost of litigation includes an opponent's legal fees in the event of failure, contingency fees are likely to be of little help in practice. The success of contingency fees in the US is, no doubt, linked to the lack of such a rule.

A potential modification to contingency fees originally suggested by Justice, and then taken up by the Law Society, is the idea of a contingency legal aid fund (CLAF). A contingency arrangement is made between the client and the fund so that a set percentage of damages recovered will be paid into the fund if the client wins. This provides a reserve from which costs in losing cases are met. The CLAF arrangement might avoid too great a direct interest by lawyers in the outcome of case, but, in a British context, its use is likely to be marginal. The availability of legal aid, speculative actions and trade union finance means that such a fund would probably be affected by the phenomenon of 'adverse selection' – that is, it would be involved only in cases where the risk of failure was too great for any other method of funding. For this reason, the Law Society rejected the idea as unworkable. Hong Kong, where CLAF has had some success, does not have a legal aid scheme equivalent to our own.

Another suggested alternative to extending legal aid is the 'no-fault' compensation scheme, which has become the subject of much academic debate and inquiry. It is not the purpose of this book to take sides in this debate, but 'no-fault' compensation in limited areas (traffic accident small claims and medical accident) will almost certainly be introduced in the future. All we would say here is that it is unlikely to provide a panacea. The experience of criminal injuries compensation proves that administrative agencies can make mistakes. Consequently, many claimants will still require advice, assistance and, sometimes, representation; an adequate legal aid system must cater for this.

An additional consideration in many personal accident cases is that of the wider public interest. Medical cases are a classic example; another is the workplace accident that reveals breaches of health and safety regulations affecting all those working there. A major flaw in the present system – which divides the 'personal' action for compensation from the inquest or inquiry which represents the 'public' stage – is that these issues tend to be ignored. In many cases, victims and their relatives are as much concerned with accountability as compensation. They wish to know why an accident happened, whose fault it was and how wrongdoers are to be held to account. Yet publicly funded legal representation is not available for attending inquests; nor, other than through green form, for making representations to the Health and Safety Executive; nor for pursuing matters through family practitioner committees or hospital complaints procedures. Remedying this requires, on the one hand, an extension of public funding (see p121) and, on the other, better training.

Both the Legal Aid Board and the Law Society need to ensure that solicitors advise those who are eligible for legal aid of its advantages. They must see that solicitors assemble evidence and prepare for court; have case-management systems which will prevent procrastination, and do not advise clients to accept offers which are clearly too low. It is essential to work towards creating a pool of solicitors who both have the expertise to handle personal injury cases effectively and are able to resist the pressures imposed by insurers.

An additional strategy to improve standards is suggested by the work of Action for Victims of Medical Accidents (AVMA). To help solicitors with the training and support they need to fight medical malpractice cases, AVMA has devised short, specialised training courses and conferences with leading lawyers and doctors practising in the field, together with support groups. Another group, Social Audit, provides a high-quality specialist service to help with the evaluation and presentation of scientific evidence. Social Audit's presence in the Opren litigation undoubtedly helped to pressure the defendant company into settlement. These small-scale experiments point to the need for more sustained 'back-up' centres, financed by grant aid, to provide specialist expertise, training and encouragement.

The particular problems of multi-party actions are too complex to be fully dealt with here. While the Lord Chancellor's Department and Legal Aid Board nominally recognise the need for, and usefulness of, group actions, both have taken a grudging approach to their funding. Thus, many of the problems encountered by the Opren claimants are likely to be replicated in future cases. This raises exactly the same problem as does the reform of matrimonial law. A co-ordinated response from the bodies involved (the Lord Chancellor's Department, Legal Aid Board and judiciary) is required. For instance, the courts must develop rules to deal with what amount to class actions. These should not be delegated to the Legal Aid Board in such a way that decisions on court procedure are controlled by rules on funding.

References

1 *Royal Commission on Civil Liability and Compensation for Personal Injury* (Pearson commission) Cmnd 7054, HMSO, 1978.
2 *Multi-Party Actions* Legal Aid Board, 1992.
3 *Report of the Review Body on Civil Justice* Cm 394, HMSO, 1988, recommendation 62.

4 The National Health Service (Compensation) Bill proposed by Rosie Barnes MP, 1990.

5 Lord Chancellor's Department *Contingency Fees* Cm 571 HMSO, 1989.

6 *Improving Access to Civil Justice* Law Society, 1987.

7 As in 1 above, Table 1, p11 and para 39.

8 *37th Legal Aid Annual Reports (1986–87)* HC 233, HMSO, 1988, p55, and Legal Aid Board *Annual Report 1991–92* HC 50, HMSO, p53.

9 Review of Financial Conditions for Legal Aid *Eligibility for Civil Legal Aid: a consultation paper* Lord Chancellor's Department, 1991, p27.

10 See D Harris and others, *Compensation and Support for Illness and Injury* Oxford Socio-Legal Studies, Clarendon Press, 1984, p317.

11 H Genn *Hard Bargaining: out-of-court settlement in personal injury actions* Oxford Socio-Legal Studies, Clarendon Press, 1987, p94.

12 Consumers Association/Law Society *Legal Expenses Insurance in the UK* 1991.

13 As in 10 above, p320.

14 Figures supplied by the Legal Aid Board, 'Appendix 2K: Analysis of Results of Legal Aid Proceedings in the Queen's Bench and in the County Court'.

15 As in 10, pp105–12.

16 Civil Justice Review *Personal Injuries Litigation* Lord Chancellor's Department, 1986, p28.

17 As in 11, p41.

18 *HL Hansard debates* 29 February 1988, cols 20–22.

19 *Consultation Paper on Multi-Party Actions* Legal Aid Board, May 1989.

20 *Report on proposals to the Lord Chancellor relating to the legal aid aspects of multi-party actions* Legal Aid Board, September 1991.

21 G Dehn 'Opren: problems, solutions and more problems' *Journal of Consumer Policy* 12, 1989, pp397–414, 409.

22 See 2 above, para 37.

23 H Genn *Meeting legal needs? An evaluation of a scheme for personal injury victims* Oxford Centre for Socio-Legal Studies and Greater Manchester Legal Services Committee, 1982.

24 'ALAS! leads to more claims' *Law Magazine* 31 March 1988, p12.

25 Information supplied by the Law Society press office to T Goriely.

26 G Chambers and S Harwood-Richardson *Solicitors in England and Wales: practice, organisation and perceptions: second report – the private practice firm* Research and Policy Planning Unit, Law Society, 1991, p37.

27 *27th Legal Aid Annual Reports [1976–77]* HC 172, HMSO, p123.

28 As in 5 above, paras 2.10 and 3.12.

CHAPTER 5

Debt

The study of publicly funded legal services available in the field of debt provides a contrast with the previous discussions of matrimonial and personal injury work. Debt is not a single, easily delineated area of law. This is clearly indicated by the way that the CAB service uses its statistics. In its 1987/88 annual report, while including debt cases under the heading 'consumer, trade and business' in the tables, NACAB referred in the text to 'consumer, debt and related'; subsequently this was reduced to 'consumer and debt'. The collection of legal aid information has shown more constancy in nomenclature, but debt statistics are still combined with those for hire purchase. A further complication in obtaining a clear view of the extent of debt as a problem is that mortgage arrears cases are often counted as a housing problem, both by the Legal Aid Board and in NACAB statistics.

The CABx's shift of emphasis reflects a very real economic change. Debt escalated during the 1980s at what, in hindsight, seems a terrifying rate. Between 1981 and 1990, the amount of outstanding consumer debt more than trebled in cash terms – rising from £15.5 billion to £52.6 billion – and more than doubled in real terms. An increasing proportion of this debt mountain was the result of credit card and finance house lending – these two sources of credit rising from 20 to 28 per cent of all outstanding debt. At the same time, the expansion of home ownership increased the number of mortgages from 6.3 million in 1981 to 9.6 million in 1991. Over the same period, the number of loans in arrears by more than six months rose from 21,500 to 159,200 and the number of repossessions jumped from 4,900 to 36,600.[1] The extent of the likely increase in unlicensed and unlawful lending is not, of course, recorded.

There are now over two million households in debt – almost double the number in 1981. More than half a million households are in serious debt to three or more creditors – in 1981, there were only 130,000 with such multiple debts.[2]

There is, of course, a fine line between being in receipt of credit and being in debt. Partly, this is a reflection of overall solvency. Well-off families are more likely to use consumer credit; poor families are more likely to be in debt, particularly with regard to basic household expenses (such as housing, fuel and water costs or local government tax), which account for two-thirds of all debts. There is a strong link between debt and households with children: single parents, large families and those with new babies are particularly vulnerable. Debt also occurs frequently in conjunction with other problems which have legal consequences, such as divorce or loss of employment.

In comparison with matrimonial or personal injury work, which have traditionally formed part of legal practice, it has taken the scale of the debt mountain of the 1980s and the depth of the recession in the 1990s to obtain recognition of the need for advice and representation in this area. The collection of different kinds of debt is regulated by a variety of procedures and the ability to negotiate these involves distinct legal skills. However, in the field of 'money advice', an area which has developed in recent years, many practitioners eschew any identification with narrow legal specialism and demand that a 'multi-disciplinary' approach is required to deal with the complex problems associated with debt.

Enforcement procedures

Debtors face a confusing variety of procedures in debt enforcement, but receive little official guidance about how the system works. Many of the procedures are punitive in nature, being based on the assumption that debtors could pay if they wanted to. But the accumulated evidence suggests that, besides finding it difficult to explain their circumstances, most debtors simply cannot afford to meet their obligations. They are, therefore, caught up in inappropriate enforcement procedures mechanisms.

According to a recent study, creditors issue court proceedings in one out of ten legally enforceable debts.[3] Enforcement proceedings usually take the form of county court default summons, the majority of which are to collect debts and are issued on behalf of companies and institutions against individuals. The number of such summonses has doubled in ten years, from 1.6 million in 1980 to 3 million in 1990.

Research for the Civil Justice Review gives a picture of the progress of debt actions.[4] When defendants receive a summons they have a choice: either admit a debt and make an offer to pay, or dispute it and put in a defence. In practice, two-thirds of defendants fail to reply at all, and judgment may be entered against them by a purely administrative process. Of the one-third of defendants who do reply to a summons, very few put in a defence, suggesting that many genuine defences – for example, that goods arrived damaged – are never put before the court.[5] Most of those who do reply make an offer to pay, which creditors usually accept. Money advisers frequently complain that defendants offer too much, leading to further default and problems for creditor, debtor and court.

Creditors have a choice about how judgments may be enforced, but by far the most usual method is a 'warrant of execution', otherwise known as sending in the bailiffs. In 1990, the county courts issued 1.34 million warrants. Although courts regard default summonses and bailiffs' warrants as routine, they are rarely so for the defendants involved. In one survey of 150 people receiving a visit from the bailiffs, one-third said that their health had suffered, one-third said that their family's health had suffered, and two people had taken drug overdoses. Twenty-eight respondents tried to borrow money to repay the debt, often at very high rates of interest, thereby compounding existing problems.[6] Debtors can apply to the court for a warrant to be suspended but, in a recent study, 80 per cent of debtors were unaware of this.[7]

Housing repossessions

A second major growth area for debt is that of housing. Many people find paying rent or a mortgage a struggle: one study found that, in March 1991, 8 per cent of all mortgages were two or more months in arrears[8] – and the situation is getting worse. Another study found that tenants face even greater difficulties in paying their rents.[9] Those who fail to keep up their mortgages or pay their rent usually receive a county court summons for possession.

Possession actions are also increasing rapidly, up from 153,870 in 1986 to 276,296 in 1990. Half are brought by mortgage lenders, around two-fifths by 'social' landlords (that is, local authorities or housing associations) and one in ten by private landlords. Most actions are for arrears: one survey found that only 5 per cent of local authority possession cases are on other grounds.[10]

A major reason for rent arrears is confusion over housing benefit. In one study, around one-third of council tenants in arrears mentioned this, and another 13 per cent raised the related problem of non-dependant deductions.[11] Most council tenants do not receive any independent advice about possession proceedings. Yet, if they did so, advisers could tell where the council is at fault or clear up confusions over benefits.

Despite the sharp rise in mortgage possessions in recent years, building societies claim that they try to avoid going to court; instead, they say that they monitor accounts regularly, establish contact with defaulters quickly and attempt a variety of 'forbearance' strategies before issuing a summons. In fact, most lenders rely on standard procedures and letters. Where agreements are reached, they tend overwhelmingly to require payment of the current mortgage plus a sum off the accumulated arrears. As most borrowers have not been able to meet the current mortgage, these agreements are rarely realistic. It is unusual for borrowers to involve outsiders, yet an adviser could explore other avenues, such as capitalising the arrears, extending the mortgage term or, at the very least, negotiating more reasonable repayment terms.[12]

Lack of information

As noted above, few defendants return the 'form of reply' that accompanies a summons, and those that are returned rarely contain any useful information. Many defendants avoid court: three-quarters of council tenants, half of private tenants and two-fifths of mortgage borrowers issued with a summons fail to attend the hearing. According to the Civil Justice Review, defendants are represented by an adviser or friend even more rarely – in only 8 per cent of cases.[13]

In the absence of any information from defendants, courts cannot perform the role legislation requires of them, or consider properly all the options available. They are unable to ensure that it is 'reasonable' to make an order or that suspended orders will not cause 'exceptional hardship', as required by the Housing Act 1985;[14] nor are they in a position to exercise discretion to suspend or postpone mortgage repossession.[15] Also, they will rarely spot which borrowers are entitled to additional protection under the Consumer Credit Act 1974.[16]

Instead, most hearings are over very quickly: one judge described them as 'purely administrative, somebody independent of the local authority to rubber stamp the document'.[17] The result is that outright orders of possession are more likely than suspended orders. The Civil Justice Review found that the former were made in 49 per cent of cases where the defendant failed to appear, compared with only 39 per cent in cases where the defendant attended the hearing and 29 per cent in cases where the defendant was represented by a third party.[18]

Even where suspended orders are made, they can be unduly harsh. Defendants are often desperate to save their homes, and may well offer to pay unrealistic sums each week. Without the time or the independent expertise available to explore a debtor's situation in detail, courts routinely accept such offers. Yet when debtors later fail to keep up payments, they may lose their rights and the landlord or lender can evict them without returning to court.

Disconnections

Historically, the most common sanction for fuel and water debts has been the threat of disconnection. Until recently, suppliers have had wide powers to disconnect debtors without external supervision; however, with the privatisation of gas, electricity and water companies, the legal position has changed. Privatised companies must now comply with licence conditions imposed by the industry regulators. For example, in 1989, the gas regulator, Ofgas, required British Gas to adopt procedures which distinguish between debtors who refuse to pay and those who are unable to do so.[19] People in genuine difficulties must now, 'where it is safe and practical to do so', be offered a pre-payment meter calibrated to take into account their ability to pay. So far, this has led to a dramatic reduction in the official number of UK gas disconnections – from 48,037 in 1988 to 18,680 in 1991.[20] However, this can contribute to another problem, that of 'self disconnection' (where there is an inability to pay through coin meters).

Since April 1990, electricity supply companies have had to abide by a similar requirement,[21] and apparently with a similar result: official electricity disconnections in England and Wales fell from over 100,000 in 1985/86, to 38,720 in 1991.[22] Consultations are now under way about introducing licence conditions on disconnections by the privatised water companies.[23]

Debt advisers have been much involved in the formulation of licence conditions. The dramatic improvement in disconnection rates since the introduction of such conditions demonstrates what can be achieved when advocates of legislative reform draw upon their experience of traditional casework.

Administration orders

Defendants often experience several enforcement actions at once, and even the best-intentioned repayment plan in relation to one debt can be thrown into confusion if another creditor's bailiff knocks on the door.

County court administration orders allow debtors to ask for all their debts to be dealt with together. Debtors then make a single payment to the court, which is distributed pro rata to all the creditors attached to the order; no creditor included in the order can take other enforcement action without the court's leave. Administration orders cannot, as yet, include fuel and water debts, which can be independently pursued through disconnections.

Debtors with administration orders find them helpful.[24] But relatively few are made – only 5,932 in 1990. Research in Birmingham found that debtors were more likely to apply for administration orders – and more likely to comply with them – if they had visited an advice agency.[25] Unrepresented debtors usually do not know about such orders or, if they do, find it difficult to deal with the complex paperwork involved.

The Courts and Legal Services Act 1990 includes reforms to improve administration orders for both debtors and creditors. The upper financial limit is to be removed and fuel and water debts are to be included. Whereas in the past such orders could extend over an inordinate length of time, sometimes for ten or more years, no administration order is to last more than three years; district judges will be empowered to make composition orders, reducing the overall amount of the debt rather than allowing the order to run on until all the original debts are paid. However, this reform is only likely to be effective if more money advisers are available to assist both debtors and the courts in implementing the reformed procedures.

Extortionate credit

In 1971, the Crowther Committee on Consumer Credit argued that some interest rates were so high as to be socially harmful.[26] In order to prevent this, the Consumer Credit Act 1974 gave courts the power to re-open credit agreements where interest payments are 'grossly exorbitant' or which 'otherwise grossly contravene ordinary principles of fair dealing'.[27] The provisions replaced the previous Moneylenders Act 1927, which established a presumption against interest rates in excess of 48 per cent.

A recent report by the Office of Fair Trading[28] shows that the Act has been little used. The OFT could trace only 15 court decisions on extortionate credit – and in all but four, the consumer had lost. Yet socially harmful credit transactions continue, and form a major problem for those borrowers locked into their provisions.

Consumers are reluctant to bring claims against backstreet lenders, which they use only as a last resort. If they complain, they jeopardise their source of credit; they may also fear violence. But it is surprising that challenges have not been made at least against secured loans with extortionate rates of interest, since these require enforcement through the courts.[29]

A major problem is the lack of legal expertise in this area. As the Office of Fair Trading pointed out, advice centres may be 'too overwhelmed with negotiations on behalf of numerous debtors' to identify the exceptional case where extortionate credit is charged.[30] Nor can the advisers in such centres, as non-lawyers, apply for legal aid to help finance the growing demand for debt advice. Money advisers may also lack the necessary legal skills to argue cases in full court. Solicitors, on the other hand, neither normally practice in this field of law nor necessarily know much about it, at least not from the point of view of debtors. The success of the Consumer Credit Legal Centre in Victoria (see p99) points to the scope for specialist legal skills to deal with this type of problem.

The role of legal aid

Full civil legal aid is not generally available for debt matters. Schedule 2 of the Legal Aid Act 1988 excludes defendants in county court proceedings from receiving assistance where the only issue is the 'time and mode of payment . . . of a debt'. Housing possession cases are not excluded specifically, though the Legal Aid Board has given differing guidance about whether it is reasonable to grant legal aid for such proceedings. In practice, solicitors rarely represent defendants.

The Civil Justice Review recommended that the Legal Aid Board should fund county court duty representation schemes, and the board recently completed a study which recommended funding for in-court services to be provided by either lawyers or other advisers.[31] Around 20 such schemes already operate on a voluntary basis in particular county courts, but it seems unlikely that the necessary finance will be forthcoming to set up a comprehensive service.

Green form advice covers debt, and, in 1991/92, the scheme dealt with 82,754 bills for debt and hire-purchase work, a low number compared with the volume of debt cases passing through the courts. Many people do not know that such assistance is available – and debtors are particularly worried by the prospect of having to pay legal bills.

In any case, even when solicitors do undertake green form debt cases, they spend very little time on them – an average of 1.4 hours.[32] This compares with the 14 hours it is estimated that money advice workers will regularly spend on a debt case.[33] Solicitors tend to focus on the single debt currently subject to legal action, explaining court proceedings, helping fill in forms and possibly advising on an offer that will be acceptable to the particular creditor. Few of them look at all the household debts or give advice about budgeting and claiming benefits.

Money advice

The advice movement has tried to fill this gap in the legal aid scheme and in the quality of advice offered by solicitors. Although most people seek help to cope with an immediate threat, such as disconnection or the bailiffs, money advice workers, who owe their techniques as much to counselling as to the law, try to go beyond this in order to get a full picture of a person's debts. They help to maximise income by claiming benefits or seeking tax rebates, and prepare a financial statement showing all income and outgoings. They then negotiate with priority creditors and suggest that any surplus is split pro rata among the others. Where a client has no money, they will try to get a debt remitted.[34]

Money advice services have grown quickly. In 1982, the National Consumer Council identified only 16 specialist services in England and Wales.[35] A more recent survey in March 1989 found 286 organisations offering some form of specialist money advice.[36] This included six independent money advice centres, 60 advisers employed in local authorities and 17 support units providing specialist training and consultancy in debt work to general agencies. The largest number (166) were based in CABx; yet, even those CABx often have only one specialist money adviser trying to meet the needs of a whole area.

Another approach to money advice is demonstrated by National Debtline, a country-wide experimental project, which aims to encourage self-help. Callers are given advice over the telephone and sent a do-it-yourself information pack. A survey showed that users tend to ring the debtline before their creditors have threatened court proceedings. Most of them then work out a personal budget, and contact at least some creditors to arrange repayment plans.[37]

There are three major problems with money advice services. First, most are inadequately staffed due to lack of resources. The March 1989 survey referred to above found that, between them, 286 organisations employed fewer than 250 full-time equivalent staff on money advice, and this included volunteers. Second, the development of money advice has put considerable strain on the generalist service offered by agencies such as the CABx. Around 13 CABx have managed to fund a money advice post only by cutting down on the number of generalist workers, and volunteers trained for money advice find that they have little time left for other work. This has highlighted the question within the CAB service of how far volunteer workers can be expected to undertake continuing work on a case or specialise in one area.[38]

Finally, there is little apparent interaction between lawyers and money advisers. Only a handful of organisations can employ both, yet their experience shows how much can be achieved by combining legal and counselling skills. Wythenshawe Law Centre, for example, has prosecuted an electricity board for harassing its debtors, set up credit unions and taken test cases on whether administration orders can include rent arrears. If legal challenges are to be taken against extortionate interest rates or unjust credit practices, greater legal skills will need to be incorporated within money advice services.

Funding

The government has so far rejected calls for greater support for providing money advice on the grounds that private sector funding should be sought from the credit industry. Over the last five years, NACAB has actively pursued voluntary donations from the credit industry, particularly for regional support units, which it regards as a high priority to improve the general level of money advice among bureaux. By 1989, against a target of £2 million a year, it had raised only £750,000, of which just £250,000 came from the private sector.[39]

In January 1990, a group of creditors and money advisers, chaired by Lord Ezra, issued a report recommending that a money advice trust be set up to seek donations of £9 million over three years.[40] But the credit industry has been reluctant to undertake this responsibility. A 1989 NACAB report showed that out of 89 institutions surveyed, only 41 felt that money advice benefited them;[41] and in 1991, the new Money Advice Trust received only £250,000 in donations from 19 different organisations, as against a target of £3 million. In 1992, Sir George Blunden, its chair, accepted that a levy might have to be enforced: 'If by the end of our third year, we don't get the growth we are expecting, we will have to approach the government and ask it to look seriously at the idea of a statutory levy', he told the *Times*.[42]

It has become clear that a levy will only work if enforced by statute, and the National Consumer Council has begun a consultation on the appropriate form this should take. The failure of the credit industry to pay for advice directly related to its field of commercial activity underlines the more general point that the subsidy for legal and advice services can realistically only come from public funds, and that any significant supplement from the private sector would require government backing through statutory enforcement.

Future action

The above suggests that any development of advice services in this field must involve more emphasis on and, therefore, funding for the generalist advice sector and specialist money advice services which currently undertake the majority of debt advice. New provisions should clearly include 'in-court' duty representation services, provided in most instances by non-lawyers and funded by the Legal Aid Board. As for the availability of specialist advice, which can both extend the work of money advisers and play a vital part in tackling problems like extortionate credit, this is unlikely to come from private practice. Even with better training and legal aid provision, solicitors will, on the whole, do no more than assist clients who have a debt problem linked to the legal matters in hand.

There is, therefore, a need to build on the role of those law centres which undertake debt work, and to increase their links with non-legal money advisers. This would be one of the functions of the community legal centres proposed in chapter 14. At the same time, some form of national specialist centre, along the lines of Victoria's exemplary Consumer Credit Legal Centre, is also required, both as a source of specialist legal advice and research for local advisers and to undertake test cases and co-ordinate national campaigns and information in this field.

References

1   Central Statistical Office *Social Trends* 22, HMSO, 1992, tables 6.15 and 8.22.
2   R Berthoud and E Kempson *Credit and Debt* Policy Studies Institute, 1992; *Patterns of Debt* Working paper 4, PSI, 1990.

3   As above, working paper 5.

4   Touche Ross management consultants *Study of Debt Enforcement Procedures* Lord Chancellor's Department, 1986.

5   M Cain, 'Who loses out in paradise island? the case of defendant debtors in the county courts' in I Ramsay (ed) *Debtors and Creditors* Professional Books, 1986.

6   R Cotterrell et al, 'The recovery of judgment debts in the county court: some preliminary results', see note 5.

7   J Phipps *Individual Judgment Debtors in One London County Court: participation and advice seeking* Centre for Commercial Law Studies, University of London, 1991.

8   'Mortgage misery deepens' *Roof* July–August 1991.

9   *Credit and Debt in Britain: first findings* Policy Studies Institute, 1990.

10 P Leather and S Jeffers *Taking Tenants to Court: a study of possession actions by local authorities* Department of the Environment, HMSO, 1990.

11 See note 10 above.

12 J Ford *The Indebted Society: credit and default in the 1980s* Routledge, 1988.

13 School of Advanced Urban Studies, University of Bristol *Study of housing cases* Lord Chancellor's Department 1987.

14 ss84 and 85 Housing Act 1985.

15 s36 Administration of Justice Act 1970.

16 ss129 and 135 Consumer Credit Act 1974.

17 J Watts, 'Local authority possession proceedings', February 1987 *Legal Action 7*.

18 See note 13.

19 Office of Gas Regulation, British Gas Licence Condition 12A.

20 Figures from the Gas Consumers Council.

21 Office of Electricity Regulation, Licence Condition 19.

22 Office of Electricity Regulation *Annual Report 1991*.

23 Office of Water Regulation *Guidelines in Debt and Disconnections* April 1992.

24 See note 4.

25 J Davies, 'Delegalisation of debt recovery proceedings: a socio-legal study of money advice centres and administration orders', see note 5.

26 *Report of the Committee on Consumer Credit* Cmnd 4596, HMSO, 1971.

27 ss137–140 Consumer Credit Act 1974.

28 Office of Fair Trading *Unjust Credit Transactions* 1991.

29 National Consumer Council *Security Risks: personal loans secured on homes* 1987.

30 See note 28, para 4.20, p23.

31 Lee Bridges *The Provision of Duty Advice Services in County Courts: report of research conducted on behalf of the Legal Aid Board* Legal Aid Board, 1991.

32 Legal Aid Board *Annual Report 1991–92* HC 50, HMSO, 1992, p79.

33 T Hinton and R Berthoud *Money Advice Services* Policy Studies Institute, 1988.

34 As above.

35 *Information and Advice Services in the United Kingdom: report to the Minister of State for Consumer Affairs* National Consumer Council, 1983.

36 T Young *Debt Advice Provision in the United Kingdom* National Consumer Council, 1990.

37 National Debtline *Caller Survey* 1990.

38 See D Forbes and S Wright *Housing Advice in Nine CABx* unpublished, 1990; Judith Citron *Citizens Advice Bureaux: for the community, by the community* Pluto Press, 1989.

39 W Stephens *The Finance Industry and Money Advice: committed or not?* Research and Development Unit, Occasional Paper 20, NACAB, 1989.

40 *The Report of the Money Advice Funding Working Party* (Chair, Lord Ezra MBE) c/o Finance and Leasing Association, January 1990.

41 See note 39.

42 'Lenders face levy for debt advice' *Times* 29 June 1992.

CHAPTER 6

Employment

Unlike debt, employment law is seen by lawyers as a discrete area of law. Indeed, the law has been crucially involved in the regulation of relations between master and servant since at least 1349, when the Ordinance of Labourers was passed in an attempt to hold down wages at a time of labour shortage. The law has been one of the main battlegrounds between trade unions and employers, and the balance in employment legislation between the rights of employers and employees has reflected the see-saw of political power.

This chapter is limited to two very specific concerns: the need for publicly funded legal services by individual employees unable to get assistance from elsewhere and the merit of intervention in individual disputes of the Equal Opportunities Commission and the Commission for Racial Equality.

Industrial tribunals

In 1949, legal aid was not seen as very relevant to employment law. This was largely regarded as the preserve of organised labour, where disputes were settled by collective action. It was only in the 1960s that the emphasis shifted to individual rights. Legislation in 1963 required employees' contractual terms to be put in writing; and in 1965, a redundancy scheme was established. This move towards more individual rights continued into the next decade. The Industrial Relations Act 1971 introduced the concept of unfair dismissal and extended the role of industrial tribunals – established under the Industrial Training Act 1964 to adjudicate on certain matters related to training[1] – to determine claims.

In 1975, the Labour government criticised the provision whereby, under the Race Relations Act 1968, only the Race Relations Board could litigate in racial discrimination cases, describing such a mechanism as 'cumbersome, ineffective and unduly paternalistic'.[2] Instead, it proposed that individual workers who had suffered discrimination should be free to bring their own cases to an industrial tribunal. This model was subsequently adopted in both the Sex Discrimination Act 1975 and the Race Relations Act 1976. Since then, Conservative governments have accelerated the trend towards individual enforcement of employment rights.

Individuals have also been increasingly thrown on their own resources in taking up employment cases through the decline of the trade union movement. Membership of trade unions has dropped from a peak of 53 per cent of the civilian workforce in 1980 to only 38 per cent in 1989.[3] At least as far as unfair dismissal claims are concerned, there is some evidence to suggest that non-unionised employees are disproportionately represented among tribunal applicants. A 1988 study showed that one-third of such claims related to those in the poorly unionised distribution, hotel and catering sector, although this accounted for only 19 per cent of all employees.[4] Poorly paid sectors of the workforce face decreasing protection, other than through individual action to enforce rights: between 1979 and 1990, for instance, wages inspectors were reduced from 158 to 71,[5] and the complete abolition of the inspectorate now seems likely.[6]

The non-unionised, low-paid employee has limited sources of assistance. Employment enquiries were the third largest element in the workload of CABx in 1990/91, accounting for 775,616 enquiries.[7] Employment green form bills paid totalled 27,594 in 1991/92, a rise of 6,673 or about 30 per cent over 1990/91.[8]

As an indication of the work of industrial tribunals, 38,988 cases were begun in 1990. The vast bulk of these related to unfair dismissal (23,251). There were also 1,813 cases alleging sexual discrimination, 1,164 racial discrimination and 588 equal pay claims. Most cases were settled before hearing (20,997), but 9,748 were heard. Of the unfair dismissal claims made in 1990/91, 1,290 resulted in an award of compensation, the median of which was £1,773; 63 reinstatement or re-engagement orders were made.[9]

Research commissioned by the Lord Chancellor and published in 1990 provides a picture of those claiming unfair dismissal who get as far as a hearing before the industrial tribunal: 31 per cent had received no advice; 36 per cent had sought advice from a solicitor; 5 per cent from a law centre; 8 per cent from a CAB, and 18 per cent from a union. It is more likely that those taking a case as far as the tribunal will have received advice than those who do not pursue their cases so far. Applicants in social class I (professionals) were most likely to have received advice from a solicitor (59 per cent) and those in social class V (unskilled manual workers) least likely (17 per cent). On the other hand, a person in class V was twice as likely to have consulted a CAB (18 per cent) than someone in class I (9 per cent).[10]

Representation at an industrial tribunal affects the chances of success. The average success rate for applicants studied in the research for the LCD was 34 per cent. The researchers found that 'where the applicant has no representation and the respondent is legally represented, the applicant's probability of success is reduced to 10 per cent. Where the applicant is represented by a non-lawyer, and the respondent is represented by a lawyer, the probability of the applicant succeeding is 18 per cent.'[11] Of the tribunals studied in the research (which also included mental health review tribunals, social security appeal tribunals and hearings before immigration adjudicators), industrial tribunals were the ones in which legal representation was of the greatest benefit: 'representation by a barrister results in the highest probability of success for either an applicant or a respondent'.[12]

The relative success of lawyers in industrial tribunals is not surprising. With employers generally legally represented, the tribunal has been moulded, to a large degree, by the lawyers appearing before it. In consequence, it has become very much like a court: along with a raised bench, oaths and set procedures, there are now no less that four separate sets of case reports which may be drawn upon – cumbersome enough for lawyers, let alone for all but the most experienced lay adviser.

The domination of lawyers within industrial tribunals raises two questions: Is it possible to develop procedures to exclude lawyers? And, if not, how should representation be provided to those unable to afford them? This book cannot address the first question in any depth, but it is worth noting that a non-lawyer mediation element, in the form of the Advisory Conciliation and Arbitration Service (ACAS), is incorporated within the industrial tribunal structure.

ACAS employs conciliation officers who make contact with both parties and investigate the possibility of settlement. Research suggests that unrepresented applicants appear to be grateful that a 'man from the tribunal' calls on them and listens to their grievance. But questions remain as to the fairness of ACAS-negotiated settlements. There is evidence to suggest widespread misunderstanding of the role of conciliation officers, who are not meant to give advice about the merits of a case and who must pass on all offers, however low. One study concluded that conciliation officers 'transmit pressures to settle which the systems contains without seeking to ameliorate them'.[13] The high proportion of cases settled before a tribunal hearing – 20,997 in 1990, almost double the number of hearings – suggests that ACAS effectively operates as a filter. It computed that the average cost of a conciliation in 1991 was £174, compared with the average cost of a tribunal hearing of £942.[14]

Because of the evident need for lawyers, industrial tribunals have been at the centre of the debate about whether legal aid should be extended to tribunals in general. Some such extension was supported by the Royal Commission on Legal Services in 1979, by the Lord Chancellor's Advisory Committee and by the Council on Tribunals.[15] The Royal Commission recommended an extension of lay representation and suggested that legal aid should be available for tribunals in seven situations, the first four of which were proposed to it by the Council on Tribunals:

- significant points of law;
- 'where evidence is likely to be so complex or specialised that the average layman could reasonably wish for expert help in assembling and evaluating the evidence and in its testing or interpretation';
- in test cases;
- 'where the deprivation of liberty or the ability of an individual to follow his occupation is at stake';
- when the amount at stake, though low, is significant to the applicant;
- when suitable lay representation is not available;
- 'when the special circumstances of the individual make legal presentation desirable or when hardship might follow if it was withheld'.[16]

In 1983, the government agreed these proposals 'in principle, subject to further consideration being given to timing and the availability of resources'.[17] However, no extensions have been implemented, other than to make ABWOR available in mental health review tribunals in 1982. The Lord Chancellor's parliamentary secretary recently said that any further extension was 'unrealistic'.[18]

If legal aid were to be extended to industrial tribunals, the statutory charge or tribunal cost rules would also need modification. The average award for unfair dismissal would be severely reduced, if not entirely eliminated, by the statutory charge because costs are awarded only exceptionally by the industrial tribunals against a losing party. Accordingly, an extension of legal aid in its present form would have relatively little effect. This is one reason why other mechanisms need to be found to extend representation to tribunals (see p118).

Race and sex discrimination

Cases involving allegations of racial or sexual discrimination are particularly difficult to present to a tribunal, and applicants proceeding on their own face tremendous problems. A survey commissioned by the Equal Opportunities Commission described the problems of the quarter of applicants alleging sexual discrimination who try to handle their own cases: 'Many applicants did not know what a hornets' nest they had disturbed. Few were prepared for the complexities, the delay, the technicalities, the absence of information and so on . . . they could often expect little informed guidance from counsellors and advisers, and . . . conciliation officers were "neutral" at best.'[19] The same problems are to be found in racial discrimination cases. Of all applicants to an industrial tribunal, those alleging racial discrimination are least likely to receive advice, most likely to withdraw and least likely to be represented.[20]

As a recognition of the difficulties, both the Equal Opportunities Commission and the Commission for Racial Equality have the power to provide assistance with legal cases – the EOC under the Sex Discrimination Act 1975 and the CRE under the Race Relations Act 1976.

CRE assistance is, in effect, a form of legal aid but it operates with a fixed total budget that places restrictions on the cases which it can assist. The CRE reported recently: 'The number of complaints increased from 1,150 in 1985 to 1,381 in 1990 . . . Though we have committed more funds to this area, given the stringent constraints upon our finances we are likely to have to refuse a larger number of applications than in the past.'[21]

For those who cannot get help from the CRE, the prospects of assistance are certainly bleak. A recent study by the Policy Studies Institute[22] found that almost two-fifths of applicants receive no advice at all, 13 per cent use a solicitor without CRE assistance, 10 per cent are helped by trade unions and 6 per cent by law centres. Those with CRE help do dramatically better than those without: only 16 per cent withdraw before the hearing, compared with more than half of unrepresented applicants; and 54 per cent of CRE-assisted applicants win contested hearings, compared with 20 per cent of those with other representation and only 2 per cent of unrepresented applicants.

The PSI study commented that although stronger cases attract representation, representation also increases the chances of success: 'indeed, legal representation appears almost a prerequisite of success'. It found several reasons for this. Unsupported applicants need to be 'exceptionally dogged and determined' in order to stay the course. Not only is discrimination law complex and little understood, success is also dependent on witnesses, statistical evidence and formal moves to obtain documents, which few unrepresented applicants can arrange. The PSI also gives several examples of tribunal chairs who were aggressive or positively discouraging. A practical effect of the dominance of the CRE is that tribunals tend to feel that those cases which the CRE has not assisted or, worse, where it has given initial advice but been unable to provide representation, are of less merit than those in which the CRE assists the applicant through to the tribunal hearing.

The CRE has made attempts to pass on its expertise. Its 'do-it-yourself' kits and courses for community relations councils appear to have had only a limited impact. But its recent work with law centres, including the funding of two posts and agreement to pay counsel fees where law centres do the solicitor's work, has been more successful. The PSI study found that law centres 'achieve results at least as good as solicitors briefed by the applicants and probably better'.

Many sex discrimination complainants, according to EOC research, are also unlikely to receive assistance. A postal survey found that only 24 per cent of the applicants in the sample had received assistance. Of those that did, 28 per cent had got help from a trade union, 20 per cent from the EOC itself, 16 per cent from a lawyer of some kind, and 7 per cent from the CAB. The researchers commented: 'The outcome of cases did not appear to be particularly affected by the *type* of applicant representation, though applicants who were unrepresented were rather more likely to settle and less likely to proceed to tribunal than those who were represented.'[23] In 1991, the EOC faced 382 requests for assistance, 257 of which related to sex discrimination; it granted assistance in 124 cases and advice in 10 others.[24]

The EOC and the CRE have derived different conclusions from their experience. The EOC places its emphasis on the need for better training of industrial tribunal members and chairs. It is not, however, convinced that the extension of legal aid to sex discrimination cases is 'either realistic or desirable'. Part of the answer, it suggests, is 'a regional structure for the commission itself to enable it to work more closely with advice agencies and voluntary groups to provide support and assistance'.[25]

The CRE, on the other hand, is firmly of the view that legal aid should be available in racial discrimination cases. It quotes with approval the statement of a Manchester industrial tribunal in the case of *Freeman v Salford Health Authority*: 'This case highlighted the necessity for applicants in discrimination cases to be properly represented. The only way that an applicant's case can be satisfactorily presented is by a properly briefed advocate. So much of an applicant's case depends upon in-depth cross-examination of the respondents' witnesses. Such a cross-examination can in most cases only be conducted by a skilled advocate. Fortunately in this case the applicant's representation was financed by the Commission for Racial Equality. Unfortunately their resources only permit them to represent in selected cases. There must clearly be a case for the availability of legal aid, with proper safeguards, in discrimination cases.'[26]

Neither the existence of a conciliation mechanism in the form of ACAS, nor out-of-court determination by a tribunal, affects the need for adequate representation. That the results of industrial tribunal hearings can be proved statistically to be affected by the incidence and type of representation available to the parties is a clear example of unequal access to justice. It is unacceptable that the powerful and the wealthy should have such a manifestly unfair advantage. The need for representation is underlined by the successful use of the very limited funding available from the CRE and the EOC. LAG's proposals for dealing with these problems are set out in chapter 14 and involve, in particular, development of the law centre model of provision. In Part III, the publicly funded legal services provided in five foreign jurisdictions are discussed, with particular attention to how those services relate to social welfare law areas such as employment.

References

1 Contracts of Employment Act 1963 and Redundancy Payments Act 1965.
2 Home Office *Racial Discrimination* Cmnd 6234, 1975, para 41.
3 Central Statistical Office *Social Trends* 22 HMSO, 1992, table 11.19.
4 M Stevens, 'Unfair Dismissal Cases in 1985–86: characteristics of parties' *Employment Gazette* December 1988, p651.
5 *Crime Without Punishment: the story behind wages council underpayment* Low Pay Unit, 1990.
6 'Wages councils attacked' *Times*, 8 July 1992.
7 *Annual Report 1990/91* NACAB, 1991.
8 Legal Aid Board *Annual Report 1991/92* HC 50, HMSO, 1992, from which all 1991/92 figures are taken unless otherwise stated.
9 Council of Tribunals *Annual Report 1990/91* HC 97, HMSO, 1991; *HC Hansard written answer* 30 June 1992, cols 542–3.
10 H Genn and Y Genn *The Effectiveness of Representation at Tribunals* LCD, 1989, p39.

11 As in 10, p99.

12 As in 10, p108.

13 L Dickens *Dismissed: a study of unfair dismissal and the industrial tribunal system* Basil Blackwell 1985.

14 Advisory Conciliation and Arbitration Service *Annual Report 1991* ACAS, 1992, p70.

15 *Annual Report of the Council on Tribunals [1983–84]* HC 42, HMSO, 1984, para 2.1–2.2 and Lord Chancellor's Legal Aid Advisory Committee *33rd Legal Aid Annual Reports [1982–83]* HC 137, HMSO, 1983, pp194–207.

16 Royal Commission on Legal Services *Final Report* Cmnd 7648, HMSO, 1979, paras 15.27–15.29.

17 Lord Chancellor's Department *The Government Response to the Report of the Royal Commission on Legal Services* Cmnd 9077, HMSO, November 1983, p18.

18 *HC Hansard oral answers*, 8 June 1992, col 18.

19 C Graham and N Lewis *The Role of ACAS Conciliation in Equal Pay and Sex Discrimination Cases* Equal Opportunities Commission, 1985, p47.

20 *Employment Gazette* May 1991, and as in 10.

21 Commission of Racial Equality *Annual Report 1990* CRE, 1992, p13.

22 C McCrudden and others *Racial Justice At Work* Policy Studies Institute, 1991.

23 As in 19, p34.

24 Equal Opportunities Commission *Annual Report 1991* EOC, 1992.

25 Equal Opportunities Commission *Equal Treatment for Men and Women: strengthening the acts* EOC, 1988, paras 4.19–4.22.

26 Commission for Racial Equality *Second Review of the Race Relations Act 1976* CRE, 1991, paras 47–56.

Part III

Systems of delivery

CHAPTER 7

The Netherlands

The Netherlands is the only country in the European Community with a legal aid system comparable to that of England and Wales. Dutch legal aid, first established in 1957, is administered directly by the Ministry of Justice, the equivalent of the Lord Chancellor's Department. At present, there is no intermediate body, though the establishment of regional legal aid councils, similar to local versions of our Legal Aid Board, are planned in forthcoming legislation.

Total expenditure on publicly funded legal services in 1989 was 281 million guilders – the equivalent of £85 million.[1] Per head of the population, this represents £5.80, around half that spent in England and Wales. Advocates receive about 82 per cent of total expenditure on legal services, reflecting a high degree of dependence on the private sector. Most of the remaining expenditure funds a network of *Buros voor Rechtshulp*. In 1989, these cost 40 million guilders (about 15 per cent of the overall legal aid budget). The *buros* combine two roles. They act as a form of law centre, giving initial advice, taking on 'welfare law' cases and acting as a point of referral. They also process legal aid applications and certificates, to some extent operating like a Legal Aid Board area office. The two functions do not co-exist easily and the proposed legislation will separate them. A relatively small amount, 7 million guilders in 1989, goes to university-based law shops, training, various legal aid organisations and trade unions.[2]

While the services provided by the *buros* are free, legal aid from private practitioners is subject to means testing and contributions from income and capital. Since 1983, a charge has been made for everyone using the civil scheme: in 1991, the minimum contribution was about £8 for advice and £50 for a court case. In practice, however, many advocates refuse to collect these charges, which have been strongly opposed by the legal profession.

Legal aid

Dutch advocates have maintained a tradition of professional responsibility towards legally aided work. In 1989, virtually every single advocate – 5,995 out of a total of 6,015 – undertook a legally aided case. But most of the work is handled by a smaller number of specialists: in 1989, only 2,000 advocates undertook more than 50 cases.[3] As a legacy of the radicalism of the 1970s, within the legal aid specialists, there is a defined sector of 'social advocates' who bring a social and political commitment to legal aid work. Their representative organisation, the *Vereniging van Sociale Advocatuur Nederland*, has about 400 members and actively campaigns for better services. In 1990, it called a day of action on legal aid remuneration; and although the original intention of withdrawing services did not occur widely, Ministry of Justice fax machines were jammed with protests.

Dutch advocates undertake many more civil than criminal cases: 257,000 civil compared with 71,100 criminal in 1989. Expenditure reflects this: in 1989, civil cases brought in 157 million guilders to private practitioners, compared with 62 million guilders for criminal cases and just under 12 million guilders for the police station duty lawyer scheme.

Proposed legislation will introduce a requirement on legal aid practitioners to register with their local legal aid council in order to be able to receive legally aided work. Conditions for such registration will be similar to those considered by the Legal Aid Board for franchises. The intention is to include requirements about the volume of work undertaken, the expertise of the lawyers concerned and the organisation of their practice.

Buros voor Rechtshulp

The *Buros voor Rechtshulp* developed out of the student-based law shops of the 1970s. There are now 20, operating out of 57 separate offices and employing 235 legal and 160 administrative staff. In 1987, 332,151 clients used their services.[4]

The *buros* are independent foundations, each governed by a board which includes local lawyers, judges and academics; there is little community involvement in their management. The work of each *buro* is agreed on the basis of an annual plan submitted to the ministry for funding. Although all *buros* undertake casework, some refer more cases to private practitioners in order to concentrate on education, outreach and law reform activities. Workers in these *buros* tend to emphasise the importance of such 'structural legal aid'.

The extent to which *buros* should be involved in law reform is a contentious issue. Although their representative organisation, *Landelijke Organisatie Buros voor Rechtshulp* (LOB), actively campaigns in this area, in practice much of this work is undertaken on its behalf by the larger *buros*, particularly those in Amsterdam, the Hague and Utrecht. Other workers, especially in the smaller *buros*, regard this approach as a relic of the past – one referred to it as 'still living in the 1970s'.

The Amsterdam *buro*, the first to be established, is the largest in the country. It employs 62 people, including 30 legal staff, in four offices, and confines its caseload to social security, employment, housing, consumer and immigration work. Its central office is open to the general public five times a week, with two morning, one afternoon and two evening sessions: there are also two advice sessions for immigrants (one for people from Turkey and the other for Moroccans). In addition, legal staff visit the city's prison to give criminal and general advice.[5]

A member of staff acknowledged that the *buro* has a problem in meeting demand. Originally, the central *buro* had been open eight hours a day, five days a week, but this created too much work for the staff to handle. Demand has also been limited by reducing publicity about the *buro*'s services. In consequence, its catchment area tends to be within a relatively small radius of its main and satellite offices.

The *buro*/advocate debate

Although *buro* legal staff have law degrees and could qualify as advocates, professional rules stop advocates from working in salaried employment. This means *buro* staff cannot represent clients in those courts where only advocates have rights of audience. Some *buro* staff resent this: the Leeuwarden *buro* has sought, so far unsuccessfully, to challenge the restriction in the courts. Many *buro* workers believe that the right to employ advocates would result in the *buros* moving further away from their radical law centre-style origins and towards a network of salaried lawyers delivering services in direct competition with private practitioners. Not surprisingly, the Order of Advocates strenuously opposes relaxation of its rules. The Ministry of Justice, however, supported Leeuwarden's challenge. One official said that dual provision of legal aid was desirable in principle because it would introduce 'a kind of concurrency' in which competition would help to hold down costs. This battle continues within the *buro* movement and outside it, but the signs are that it will be resolved in favour of advocates being employed in *buro*.

Advice agencies

The Netherlands has the equivalent of a CABx network. There are 90 *raadslieden* or local information and advice centres, run mostly by local authorities. In total, the federation of *raadslieden* (FIRA) estimates that there are about 250 paid information and advice workers. In just under half of cases, *raadslieden* give only information or advice, and in a further two-fifths, assistance is limited to writing letters or filling in forms. The *raadslieden* are not seen by the Ministry of Justice as part of legal aid provision – an attitude which FIRA complains about, deploring the 'walls between ministries'.[6]

Eligibility and scope

Criminal legal aid is provided free to defendants in custody and to those on remand 'who cannot afford a lawyer'. Civil legal aid eligibility levels, set by statute in 1981, are linked to statutory rates of maintenance which are, in turn, indexed to wages. This protection has been sufficient to see off attempts by the Ministry of Justice to cut eligibility. The ministry estimates that around 70 per cent of the population is currently eligible, a significantly higher proportion than in England and Wales (see p24).

The relatively small expenditure on criminal legal aid may be a reflection of the Dutch inquisitorial system and low crime rates, as well as the low level of remuneration (see below). A duty police scheme, administered by the *buros*, works on a similar basis to that in England and Wales, except that it does not operate after about 9pm and the lawyer is requested by fax rather than telephone.

The four largest areas of civil legal aid work undertaken by private practice in 1989 were family (34 per cent), property and contract (14 per cent), social security (11 per cent) and labour law (10 per cent). The *buros* did most work in social security (18 per cent), labour law (18 per cent), housing (15 per cent) and property/contract (13 per cent), reflecting their specialist role in relation to social welfare law.

One of the most rapidly growing areas of legal aid advice for both private practitioners and *buros* concerns asylum-seekers. In 1984, there were 9,010 contacts with *buros* in this category of work and 10,140 cases assigned to private practitioners. By 1989, the number of contacts with *buros* had grown to 17,700 and the number of cases assigned to private practitioners had risen to 23,670. Asylum-seekers are placed in camps outside the main centres of population. The Order of Advocates and the *buros*, which combine to provide a special advice scheme, have vigorously opposed Ministry of Justice attempts to deprive these people, which it terms 'illegal' immigrants, of assistance.

Cost and remuneration

Debates about costs and remuneration in the Netherlands have a familiar ring. The Dutch legal aid scheme, like that of England and Wales, is demand led. The Ministry of Justice is concerned at the rise in expenditure, which has roughly doubled since 1979. The increased cost is largely a reflection of an increasing caseload: civil cases, for example, rose from 219,100 in 1984 to 257,400 in 1989 and criminal cases from 46,600 to 71,100. Remuneration rates, on the other hand, have not risen; in fact, they were cut by 10 per cent in relation to civil cases in 1981 and have not been increased for crime or civil work since then. The Order of Advocates estimates that, between 1981 and 1991, there was a real fall in remuneration rates of about 28 per cent. Payment is by way of fixed fees, which makes the failure to uprate remuneration levels a particularly effective way of holding down costs – as is clear to the Lord Chancellor's Department.

The Dutch legal aid system differs from the British model, notably in its use of salaried services through the *Buros voor Rechtshulp*. In some ways, however, it is very similar. Though the Dutch have maintained an enviably high level of legal aid eligibility, at least in civil cases, current concern with the related questions of quality, remuneration and coverage are common to both jurisdictions.

References

1   The material for this chapter was collected by Tamara Goriely and Roger Smith during a visit to the Netherlands in April 1991. An exchange rate of 3.3 guilders to £1 has been used.
2   Figures of legal aid expenditure were given in an interview with Wouther Meurs and Peter Levenkamp of the Ministry of Justice.
3   Figures supplied by the *Nederlandse Orde van Advocaten* and given in an interview with Ms Lineke Minkjan, secretary with responsibility for legal aid.

4   Figures given in interview with Ms Rita Braspenning of the *Landelijke Organisatie Buros voor Rechtshulp*.

5   *Buro voor Rechtshulp Amsterdam Jaarverslag 1988–1989* and information given in interview with Bernard de Leest of the Amsterdam *buro*.

6   Information given in interview with Ms Ella Boere-Bossinger, co-ordinator of *Federatie Instituten Raadslieden* (FIRA).

CHAPTER 8

Ontario

Legal aid in Ontario began as a voluntary scheme in 1951, and was put on a statutory footing in 1967. The Ontario Legal Aid Plan (OLAP), administered by the Law Society of Upper Canada, delivers services through two different types of provision. There is a 'certificated' scheme using private practitioners, derived from the model in England and Wales, and there is a network of clinics.[1] A separate scheme provides legal services to native peoples in the 'remote north' of the province.

Legal aid expenditure in 1989/90 was $173.8 million (about £80 million). Of this, $22 million (13 per cent of total budget, a roughly similar proportion to that paid in the Netherlands to *Buros voor Rechtshulp*) was spent on legal clinics. The sources of funds were as follows:[2]

	$m
Ontario government	68
Federal government	58
Federal government grant for refugee work	2
Interest on client accounts	36
Client contributions	9
Costs, awards, etc	5
Law Society	4

The Law Society contribution derives from a compulsory $175 (£80) levy on each member of the legal profession, negotiated in 1986 between the Society and the province's Attorney General. It is regarded as a contribution towards defraying the administrative costs of OLAP, which totalled $17 million in 1989/90.

Legal aid work

The Law Society administers the certificated legal aid scheme through 47 area offices. Though based on the system in England and Wales, the area offices have considerably more autonomy: one observer described them as 'medieval fiefdoms'. The scheme is subject to eligibility rules (levels have not been increased since 1989), but the large measure of discretion in the hands of the area director means that adequate estimates of the population eligible for legal aid cannot be made.

Criminal legal aid is free for those with incomes below a certain level: in 1991, this was equivalent to about 150 per cent of the long-term welfare support rate but lower than the minimum wage. There is no mandatory free limit for civil legal aid, although the criminal limit is often followed. The upper limit for both criminal and civil cases rests explicitly with the area director's discretion. An official explained: 'There is no hard-drawn upper limit. We take into account the matrimonial home and look at both actual and normal expenditure and income.'

As in England and Wales, criminal work dominates the scheme. The 1989/90 figures for certificated cases illustrate this as follows:

	Costs	*Completed cases*
Criminal	$71million	64,297
Civil	$42million	43,000
Advice only	$138,771	1,035

In the same year, private practitioners received about $131 million from legal aid (including around $21 million for various forms of duty schemes).

Comparatively fewer practitioners participate in the scheme than in England and Wales. A Law Society official stated: 'Ontario has about 23,000 lawyers, of whom 10,000 undertake some legal aid work. Most of this, however, is concentrated in the hands of about 1,200.' He admitted to some prejudice among clients about legal aid: 'A lot of people prefer to pay even if they can get a certificate. They have the perception of a better service.'

The Law Society has reluctantly employed duty counsel on a salaried basis – to the tune of about $750,000 in 1989/90 – to cover some of the busier provincial courts (equivalent to magistrates' courts). This has exposed the Society, as both administrator of the legal aid scheme and representative of its members, to a conflict of interest, which was admitted by one officer in the following terms: 'It is a hot issue about

whether this should expand. Salaried lawyers are cheaper but the private
Bar wants the work.'

Community legal clinics

The legal clinics, which numbered 67 in April 1991, are formally
administered under the Ontario Legal Aid Plan and, thus, the Law Society
of Upper Canada. In practice, however, they achieve a measure of
independence by having a separate administrative body, known as the
Clinic Funding Committee. The CFC has five members: three appointed
by the Law Society and two by the Attorney General, and at least one
representative from each must have been 'associated with a clinic'. It has
its own staff of ten under its own director.[3]

The legal clinics are of three basic types. There are the 'multi-service'
clinics linked to other organisations – for example, the York Community
Services, where legal, health and social services are all provided from one
base. There are also about a dozen province-wide 'specialty' clinics, which
focus on specific areas, such as the environment, landlords, the elderly and
the handicapped. These clinics have different ways of working. The
Advocacy Resource Center for the Handicapped, for example, is
orientated towards litigation and has taken a number of cases on Canada's
relatively new Charter of Rights. The Advocacy Center for the Elderly, on
the other hand, focuses more on campaigning and education – for
instance, it has worked to force the issue of abuse of the elderly into the
public arena.

Most clinics are, however, in the third category: they are community-
based, with the intention of providing services unavailable under the
certificated scheme, within a defined catchment area. The clinic funding
staff has a provisional plan for a network of 90 community legal clinics to
cover the whole province. Recently, the network has expanded at the rate
of two or three a year: as the Ministry of the Attorney-General agrees
extra funding, groups hoping to establish a centre bid for funds.

The CFC requires community legal clinics, as autonomous bodies, to
have a board of directors 'which includes persons belonging to the
community which the clinics serve'. Generally, these boards contain a
large number of professional people, but a worker from the clinic in
Thunder Bay illustrated the flexibility of this type of provision and its
ability to represent the interests of a local community: 'A group of native
people . . . put in an application for a native people's clinic. They were
told that it would have to be a general clinic. They said "OK", thinking

that it would be better to have something rather than nothing . . . we now have a real clinic with a board that is all native. The name of the clinic is Objibwe for "everyone" but you have to speak Ojibwe to understand that. Out of a population which is around 12 per cent native, most government offices get 3 to 5 per cent of native people coming to them. Native people don't go to offices much. Our proportion is about 40 per cent.'[4]

The following is a description of the six main areas of the work of clinics set out by the Ontario Legal Aid Plan in 1990:[5]

1 *Summary advice and information*
Information and advice in a variety of legal areas is provided by clinic staff to over 100,000 people per year. This service is similar to that provided by civil duty counsel in that no financial eligibility testing of clients is generally required.

2 *Referrals*
Over 60,000 people a year are referred by clinics to other agencies or lawyers, thus ensuring that they have access to other appropriate services. Over 3,000 are direct referrals to the Legal Aid Plan's certificate programme or to lawyers in private practice; the remainder are referred to a variety of social service and community agencies.

3 *Client representation*
Clinics provide traditional legal services in areas of poverty law to over 30,000 people a year, including advocacy before the courts and administrative tribunals, such as the Workers' Compensation Appeals Tribunal, the Social Assistance Review Board . . . Clinic lawyers engage in appellate work at all levels of the court system.

4 *Public legal education*
Clinics have a mandate to provide legal education to the low-income communities they service, and produce a wide variety of publications, pamphlets, video presentations and oral programs. Community Legal Education Ontario is a specialty clinic funded to produce public legal education materials for clinics and their clients.

5 *Law reform*
Clinics have a specific mandate to provide legal services 'designed solely to promote the legal welfare of a community'. Clinics therefore act on behalf of client groups, or the low-income community generally, to protect and promote their legal interests before a variety of public decision-making bodies, such as municipal councils, legislative committees and public commissions. Law reform is also initiated through test case litigation.

6 *Organising and community development*
Clinics provide specialized services to assist people to organize themselves into groups able to protect or promote their legal interests, such as tenants' associations or self-help groups for injured workers. Clinics also provide

legal assistance to groups initiating community development projects, such as housing projects for low-income people, and training programs for social assistance recipients.

A few community-based clinics perform a fourth function: linked to university law departments, they also provide training for students. The best funded clinic, Parkdale Community Legal Services, occupies a special place in the legal clinics' past history and current provision. Established in 1971 as the first clinic in Ontario, it is linked to the Osgood Hall Law School. The specially designed premises it now occupies, which incorporate a large area for students to work in, are situated in the run-down area of Parkdale rather than in the middle-class university area. The clinic delivers legal education to students for periods of four to eight months, at the same time as providing the services expected of any community legal clinic. Its services are organised into four teams: landlord and tenant, workers' compensation, family/welfare and immigration.[6]

Private practice and the clinics

A 1978 report on the community legal clinics stated that their relationship with the private profession was harmonious: 'There has been much co-operation between the two branches of legal aid and essentially no competition between the clinics and the private Bar.'[7] This has continued to be largely the case. There is overlap in immigration work, where both clinics and private practitioners act on a certificated basis. However, this appears to be unproblematic: a member of the clinic funding staff referred to the clinics and the private bar as having 'reached a modus vivendi' in this area.

Conflict could, however, occur in the future. The Ontario government has established a review of certificated legal aid to look for cuts, and the clinics may be seen as some form of alternative provision, providing the same kind of 'concurrency' sought after by Dutch Ministry of Justice officials. In a move reminiscent of the Leeuwarden *Buro voor Rechtshulp* challenge (see p77), one community legal clinic made a bid to undertake matrimonial cases because of a dearth of local private practitioners willing to do so.[8] This move has been repulsed by the Law Society for the time being because it was able to establish a pilot legal advice scheme to entice private practitioners to provide matrimonial advice. This scheme, which is so closely modelled on that of England and Wales that it too has its 'green form', represents a good example of history repeating itself: it was the potential threat of law centres which propelled the Law Society into demanding a legal advice scheme in England and Wales (see p7).

The clinics have escaped relatively unscathed in the current recession, not least because of the strong cross-party political support they attract in the provincial parliament. They have continued to grow at roughly the rate of two or three a year. But, as the numbers increase, so the relationship between the independent clinics and the CFC and its staff raises more contradictions. At the same time, the central role of the CFC staff is growing – for example, a resource office is being established, which will expand its training and support role, providing the incentive for greater co-operation. The clinics are required to report in detail on their work and the clinic funding staff have developed detailed mechanisms for seeking to balance local autonomy with central accountability. An extract from the list of their performance evaluation criteria is included in appendix 2.

The clinics provide services in social welfare law in a way that combines casework, education and law reform activity. The specialty clinics function as pressure groups in the same way that the Child Poverty Action Group does in this country. The link between some of the clinics and universities has provided a solid base for legal education which has often been missing in the UK. Ontario's clinics are the model for the 'community legal centres' advocated in chapter 14.

References

1   The information on which this chapter is based was collected during a visit by Roger Smith in April 1991. The exchange rate has been taken as $2.15 = £1.

2   The information on certificated legal aid comes from the Law Society of Upper Canada Ontario Legal Aid Plan *1990 Annual Report* and interviews with Law Society officials.

3   The information on clinics comes from Law Society of Upper Canada Ontario Legal Aid Plan *Community Legal Clinics Annual Report 1989–1990*, from discussion with a number of the CFC staff including Ms Joana Kuras and Ms Stephanie Thomas, and from an interview with Ms Thea Herman, member of the CFC.

4   Interview with Rick Atkinson.

5   Ontario Legal Aid Plan *Community Legal Services Directory* 1990, pp3–4.

6   Interview with staff at Parkdale including Ms Phyllis Gordon.

7   Commission on Clinic Funding *Report* 1978, p8.

8   Interview and correspondence with Terry Hunter, Simcoe Legal Services.

CHAPTER 9

Quebec

In the early 1970s, Quebec made a political commitment to spend significant amounts of government money on publicly funded legal services.[1] This initiative was influenced by developments in the US. The name chosen for the body set up in 1972 to administer legal aid was the *Commission des Services Juridiques* echoing that of the US Legal Services Corporation; and the emphasis on public education and law reform reflected the American, rather than British, model. Another influence, explicitly referred to by ministers at the time, was the idea of a national legal service akin to a national health service. Legal aid was, and has remained, free to recipients who meet the eligibility criteria.

The initial proposal – for a fully salaried scheme with no involvement from private practitioners – was fended off by the legal profession. Clients must usually go to the *commission* for a preliminary assessment of their case, but their right then to choose either a salaried lawyer employed by the *commission* or a private practitioner has been adopted as a fundamental principle of the scheme. The retention of this choice is a major difference between the Quebec scheme and those established in Australia (discussed in the next chapter). Quebec does not have a completely fixed annual budget, and to this extent, its scheme is in tune with the demand-led nature of the legal aid scheme in England and Wales.

In 1989/90, Quebec spent $80 million (£37 million) on legal services: 51 per cent came from the federal government and 49 per cent from the provincial government.[2] Cases were divided between private practitioners, who received a total of $23 million in legal aid costs, notaries (dealing with property matters) and staff lawyers on the following basis:

	% of cases	Number
Private practitioners	36	87,913
Commission lawyers	61	151,175
Notaries	3	6,765
Total	100	245,853

Of the total number of cases handled by lawyers (excluding those involving notaries), 59 per cent were civil and 41 per cent criminal. The proportion of cases handled by private practitioners was 37 per cent overall but varied according to the type of case – 29 per cent in family law, 24 per cent in non-matrimonial civil and 47 per cent in criminal cases.

As in Ontario's certificated scheme, the provision of advice is given very little priority: a *commission* official explicitly stated that the policy was to concentrate on representation. But, in contrast to Ontario, this situation is not modified by a network of law or advice centres. Although the legislation governing the *commission* allows services to be provided by law centres, there are only two (in Hull and Pointe Saint Charles, Montreal), both of which were set up independently, before the legal aid scheme got underway.

Legal aid work does not play a significant part in private practice. In 1989/90, only 20 per cent of Quebec's advocates – 2,671 out of 13,094 – received any legal aid payment and the average was only $7,547. Only six advocates received more than $150,000, which was said to be possible only by concentrating on multiple criminal cases, heard in the same court, at the same time and where all the pleas were guilty.

Commission des Services Juridiques

The *commission* is organised through 11 regional corporations, known as *centres communautaires juridiques* (community legal centres). These each operate local *bureaux d'aide juridiques* (legal aid offices). The regional corporations have provision for local committees 'to advise . . . on the needs of economically underprivileged persons', but these bodies have little power. This absence of local involvement may have led to a lack of sensitivity on the part of the *commission* to the needs of some communities, in particular those of Quebec's native peoples. A *commission* official admitted that a number of initiatives designed to deliver services to native peoples – none of which had involved local people from the targeted communities in their management – had been closed for lack of use. This contrasts with the operation of Ontario's clinic system, as demonstrated by the clinic in Thunder Bay (see p83).

In 1989/90, the *commission* employed 383 advocates, 536 other staff and 39 articled clerks, distributed among 114 full-time and 41 part-time offices. Sixty-two per cent of the cases taken by staff advocates related to civil matters, with family law cases constituting just under half of them. Although criminal work accounted for a smaller proportion of the *commission*'s workload than that of private practitioners, *commission* lawyers handled a higher number of such cases – 57,000 as opposed to 41,000.

The *commission* ensures very tight control over its staff advocates: working conditions are highly regulated and workloads carefully monitored.[3] In 1989/90, advocates worked, on average, 1,060 'chargeable' hours, had an active caseload of 426 and devoted 2.08 hours to each case. Salaries, based on seniority and merit, ranged from just under $30,000 to just over $70,000, and the average length of service was a creditable 13 years.

Because clients can choose between a *commission* advocate and a private practitioner for the same type of case, it is possible to look at the relative costs. The *commission*'s 1989/90 figures show that the average cost per case undertaken by a staff advocate was $183.08, compared with $249.06 for a private practitioner. But it is difficult to know how useful this comparison is. Senior figures in Quebec's Bar argue that like is not being compared with like and that *commission* advocates can manipulate case figures in a way not open to a private practitioner who receives cases on referral. However, a committee of the Canadian Bar Association, thereby largely representative of private practice interests, came to the conclusion that, 'having . . . noted some possible explanations of the discrepancies, the fact remains that the Quebec data consistently demonstrate that cost-per-case for staff lawyers is lower than for private practitioners, although the size of the cost differential may be less significant than the summary data suggest and, in many instances, negligible'.[4]

Public legal education

The statutory remit of the *commission* includes a commitment to 'promote the development of information programmes to economically underprivileged persons on their rights and obligations'; and one of the *commission*'s great successes has been in the field of public legal education.[5]

A small but very effective information department has developed a number of ways of educating the public about legal rights. This includes a continuing legal information radio programme which is transmitted by 110 French-language stations throughout Quebec. Such is its success that it has been used by a number of other ministries and government bodies to disseminate their own information. The department also produces a newspaper column which is published regularly in a number of daily and weekly newspapers.

For 14 years, the information department has produced '*Justice pour tous*', a television series of 26 programmes a year which dramatises issues about legal rights. Based on a group of characters centred around a restaurant, this has dealt with problems such as the legal issues relating to ski-ing accidents, faulty septic tanks and dangerous driving. These programmes are also distributed as videos and have, for instance, been shown in public shopping places during campaigns by lawyers' organisations to increase legal awareness.

The information department produces a range of attractive information in written form, distributing several thousand brochures and folders as part of an outreach programme that also involves it in providing legal information at fairs and trade shows. The effectiveness of the *commission*'s information work is undoubtedly aided by the fact that its director of information is a radio personality in his own right and is sufficiently energetic to host a popular weekday morning radio show before coming to work. Nevertheless, the *commission*'s commitment to innovative educational approach over a sustained period of time has been impressive.

Eligibility and cost

The problem with legal aid in Quebec is the low level of eligibility. The Legal Aid Act 1972, which established the scheme, grants eligibility to those who are 'economically underprivileged'. Initially, the *commission* had power to set eligibility levels, but this was ceded to the government in 1982. Except for one rise, which applied only to families, levels have not changed since 1981, and are now below the minimum wage.

The Ministry of Justice provided LAG with an informal estimate of eligibility at 32 per cent of the population. This is disputed by Yves Lafontaine, president of the *commission* until 1990, who reckons 15 per cent to be a more accurate figure. There is some suggestion that *commission* lawyers bend the rules and that at least some of the 20 per cent of assisted people recorded as having no income at all are, in fact, over the eligibility levels.

Increasingly concerned at the failure of the government to uprate eligibility, Yves Lafontaine wrote in his 1989/90 report: 'Without the needed indexation of the eligibility criteria, legal aid becomes a special service to people on welfare. That is a far cry from the original legislative intent . . . the poor as a group do not have the capacity to push their agenda . . . in sufficiently sustained and visible ways to force issues affecting them to prominent places on the ministerial agenda . . . It increasingly seems that the only way to explode the issue would be to stage a hunger strike or a lawsuit.'[6] Not long afterwards, Yves Lafontaine was dismissed from his post, and the *commission*'s next annual report contained only a passing reference to low eligibility levels.[7]

The *commission* has been hit severely by cuts in its resources. Its annual report still details the education, organising and reform work of each of its offices as a reflection of the priority given to placing casework in the context of other activities. However, staff are effectively expected to undertake much of this in their own time.

The budget for information work was recently halved, to $200,000. It is too early to see the effects of this on the range of material which the *commission* currently provides, but they cannot be insignificant. Equally, the future of its strategic work is uncertain. To enable a *commission* lawyer to work on a major test case, Yves Lafontaine operated a rudimentary mechanism to allow the deployment of additional resources. It is not yet clear how long a commitment to create the space for such challenges will survive his departure.

On the other hand, Quebec may renew its commitment to legal aid. A government-appointed committee has recently delivered a detailed analysis of how this could be developed.[8] It found that the basic structure of the legal aid system was sound but starved of resources. It proposed a major increase in eligibility, to be paid for largely by the introduction of contributions for those above minimum levels of income and capital. Its recommendations were still under consideration in the summer of 1992.

References

1 The information on which this chapter was based by was collected during a visit by Roger Smith in April 1991.

2 Commission des Services Juridiques *18th Annual Report, 31 March 1990;* and interviews with a number of *commission* officials.

3 Work conditions in Montreal were regulated by a 64-page *Convention collective entre le centre communautaire juridique de Montréal et le syndicat des avocats de l'aide juridique de Montréal* 1991.

4 National Legal Aid Liaison Committee of the Canadian Bar Association *Legal Aid Delivery Models: a discussion paper* CBA, 1987, p39.

5 Legal Aid Act (R.S.Q. Chapter A-14).

6 As 2 above, p24.

7 Commission des Services Juridiques *19e rapport annuel 31 mars 1991.*

8 Groupe de travail sur l'accessibilité à la justice *Jalons pour une plus grand accessibilité à la justice* Gouvernement du Québèc Ministère de la Justice, 1991.

CHAPTER 10

Australia

Legal aid in Australia was first developed on a significant scale during the radical government of Gough Whitlam in the 1970s. Despite the federal structure, each state is a separate jurisdiction and has its own system of legal services (though these do not differ as markedly as in the Canadian provinces). The level of provision is, however, uneven. This study is limited to the legal aid schemes in New South Wales and Victoria, the two states that spend the most on legal aid.[1]

Australia, like Canada, has an indigenous population. The Royal Commission into Aboriginal deaths in custody has raised awareness of the severely disadvantaged situation of Aboriginal people, not only in relation to the criminal justice system but to white society more generally. Special arrangements, to some extent under Aboriginal management, outside of the mainstream state schemes, have been set up to provide legal aid on a different basis to that available to the rest of the population. These are administered completely separately and raise very different issues which we have not attempted to consider here.

The legal aid commissions

A federal system is almost bound to result in some measure of friction between national and state governments, in relation to both resources and power, and publicly funded institutions inevitably get caught up in these conflicts from time to time. The legal aid commissions in Australia are no exception.

Originally, the commissions dealt only with matters which came within state jurisdiction; legal aid for commonwealth law was handled by the Australian Legal Aid Office (ALAO). In the 1980s, state provision and the ALAO were merged and the commissions now receive both state and commonwealth funding. Consequently, they can find themselves caught between conflicting political pressures – in 1991, for example, when drawing up its annual budget, the New South Wales Legal Aid Commission found itself in the crossfire between a Labour commonwealth government and its own state government, controlled by the Liberal party. Commonwealth government pressure can also be exerted at a bureaucratic level through the Office of Legal Aid and Family Services (the commonwealth department responsible for legal services). The commonwealth has two nominees on most commissions – one is often a political appointment and the other a civil servant of some kind.

Membership and aims

The ten commissioners of the New South Wales Legal Aid Commission must include the following: two nominees from the commonwealth government; nominees from the state government, the Bar Association, the Law Society and the Labour Council; representatives of the community legal centres and 'consumer and community welfare interests'; and the commission's director. Victoria's list of commissioners is very similar, but also includes a staff nominee and a nominee from the Ministry of Community Services, taken from names submitted by the Victoria Council of Social Services.[2]

By statute, the principal function of the New South Wales commission is 'to provide legal aid and other legal services'. It has far wider powers than the Legal Aid Board, including that of setting levels of financial eligibility. Other functions include a commitment 'to initiate and carry out educational programmes designed to promote an understanding by the public, or by sections of the public, of their rights, powers, privileges and details under the laws of New South Wales'.

In its own mission statement, the commission stresses this educational role, as well as an orientation towards law reform. It commits itself 'to assisting disadvantaged people to understand, protect and enforce their legal rights and interests and to promote access to the legal system', and includes within its aims 'participating vigorously in and actively promoting law reform'.

The Victoria commission's statutory function and mission statement are similar. It aims 'to ensure that justice is obtained by those in need by providing, in a responsible, equitable and caring manner, high quality legal assistance, duty lawyer services, advice, information and education and by promoting the reform of laws and procedures that inhibit justice' and spells out more extensively than does New South Wales its commitments beyond advice, assistance and representation:

Community Legal Education
To enable the community, sections of the community, or individuals to evaluate the significance of the law and the legal system in any given set of circumstances and to act accordingly.

Law Reform
To assist in monitoring, particularly in those areas most relevant to disadvantaged persons, the effect of the law and the legal system upon the community or sections of it or individuals and to initiate or respond to proposals for law reform.

Community Legal Centres
To provide funding for, assist and monitor the development of independent community-based legal aid services to enable them to meet the needs of their communities.

Research and Development
To conduct and/or promote research into community needs relevant to legal aid services, policies and practices including developing proposals (for example, for alternative dispute resolution programmes).

The emphasis on education and reform is shared by most Australian commissions. Particularly interesting to a British observer is their express commitment to the latter. The director of the South Australian Legal Aid Commission, noting the widespread involvement of commissions in law reform initiatives, told an audience in February 1992: 'Commissions . . . have a very important role to play in law reform. Many commissions are actively working with courts and justice agencies to improve and streamline the efficiency of the courts system. This process has dual benefits for commissions and their clients. Firstly, it ensures that the system becomes simpler and less shrouded in mystery. Secondly, as a result of greater efficiencies, legal representation for clients becomes less expensive for commissions, thereby releasing funds for "preventative" advice and education programmes.'[3]

Income and expenditure
An agreement between the commonwealth and state governments divides financial responsibility between them for funding the legal aid commissions – the total amount dictated by the state government's contribution – plus whatever the commissions raise themselves in revenue from costs and contributions. In 1989/90, the division was set at 55/45 per cent respectively. The income of the New South Wales Legal Aid

Commission was $Aus69 million (£29 million). The sources were as follows:

	% contribution
Commonwealth government	43.5
State government	26.4
Contributions and costs	13.4
Statutory interest account	10.2
(interest on client account)	
Interest on investments	3.2
Other	3.3

The equivalent figures for Victoria's total income in 1989/90 of $68 million were:

Commonwealth government	38.9
Solicitors guarantee fund	30.6
State government grant	2.8
Contributions and costs	22.9
Interest on investments	3.7
Other	1.1

The figures show the importance of a contribution to cost from the use of the surplus on solicitors' guarantee (indemnity) funds and interest on client account.

Provision of services

A distinctive feature of the Australian commissions is their autonomy. Within a fixed budget, they can decide how services should be delivered and money spent. Both the Victoria and the New South Wales commissions spent more than half their budgets in 1989/90 on services provided by private practitioners – 58 per cent in New South Wales and 61 per cent in Victoria.

Nevertheless, legal aid is a considerably smaller source of income for Australian lawyers than for those in England and Wales. Research commissioned by the National Legal Aid Advisory Committee showed that, in 1986, the total legal aid budget 'was less than 5 per cent of the gross income of the legal services industry'.[4]

Moreover, the distribution of work is uneven. The presence of commission branch offices in many urban areas means that there is relatively little need to refer work to private practitioners. By contrast, the absence of branch offices elsewhere leads to a dependence on private practitioners – and according to a commission official in New South Wales, 'legal aid is vital for many suburban and country firms'. The commission has a small number of contracts with practitioners in remote areas to deliver local services; ensuring compliance and adequate standards has, however, been a problem.

The distribution, in terms of areas of law, is roughly the same in both states, and reflects the policy of keeping the majority of criminal cases in-house. Thus, in New South Wales during 1989/90, only 44 per cent of indictable crime (2,300 cases) went to private practitioners, and an even smaller proportion (38 per cent, representing just 200 cases) of work involving administrative 'social welfare' law. On the other hand, private practice handled 86 per cent (1,100 cases) relating to civil law generally.

Both states have a central headquarters and network of branch offices from which services are delivered. Victoria, for instance, had ten branch offices in June 1991. The head of its regional offices division reported a clear correlation between the presence of a branch office and the level of legal aid use: 'We can see from our computer records the effect of putting in a legal aid office. For instance, in Bendigo we recorded 1,300 referrals steadily for three years. After a local office was established there, the number of cases jumped to 2,300.' New South Wales, a larger state, had a network of 19 branches in 1991.

New South Wales commission policy in criminal cases is to provide duty representation in the lower criminal courts and to act, if it has the resources available, through salaried lawyers (but using barristers as advocates) in the higher criminal courts. As a cost-saving measure, representation is not usually granted at all for the equivalent of committal proceedings (except for murder and some other serious cases). In civil cases, the client can choose between a salaried or private practice lawyer.

Victoria has a similar attitude towards criminal cases. A breakdown of case assignments (similar to a legal aid certificate) for 1989/90 shows that of a total of 36,321 cases, 22,393 involved crime and 33.1 per cent of these were handled in-house. Civil matters accounted for 4,205 cases, 13.9 per cent of which were dealt with by salaried lawyers, as were 10.1 per cent of the 9,723 family cases.

Eligibility and scope

The problem with the Australian model of provision is that commissions have fixed budgets, and these are set too low. The effect of this is that liability for the costs of a large case can have disastrous effects on the funds available for other cases. In 1990/91, Victoria's commission spent a total of $1.4 million on just three criminal 'super trials'. In the event, it was largely reimbursed for these exceptional costs on a special basis from the state government. However, its potential exposure to such large costs led it to take the decision that 'in criminal cases likely to cost more than $200,000' it would not grant legal aid 'unless additional government funding was received for this purpose'.[5] On a more routine basis, shortage of funds restricts the scope of legal aid in both states. For instance, neither has a duty police station scheme and New South Wales has a policy of not granting legal assistance in family law cases that only involve property.

Comprehensive information is not available in either state on the level of eligibility as a proportion of the population. Victoria, however, produces an annual 'profile' of legally aided clients from a survey of 1,200 applicants which gives some indication of their general poverty. In 1990/91, 75 per cent of all assisted persons had incomes below the accepted poverty line, 46 per cent had net assets of less than $500, and 25 per cent were in 'a net debt position'. Figures from an equivalent survey in New South Wales showed a similar trend: 74 per cent of assisted persons were in receipt of benefits, only 13 per cent were in paid employment and 75 per cent had $100 or less in savings.[6]

Such information has policy consequences. The director of the Victoria commission said: 'With almost 80 per cent of our clients living below the poverty line, there is little point [in cutting financial eligibility].' Instead, Victoria was recently forced to limit the scope of legal aid further. It decided not to pay for what are sometimes called 'crash and bash' road accident claims – while, at the same time, trying to persuade the government to set up a small claims operation for these or to implement compulsory third party property insurance. The commission also raised its lower limit on legal-aided small claims from $2,500 to $5,000.

Community legal centres

Both states have a network of community legal centres: in 1991, New South Wales had 26 and Victoria 40. Australia, as a whole, had 104, the largest group (46) being jointly funded by the commonwealth and state governments, largely through the legal aid commissions.[7]

The first to be established in Australia was Redfern Legal Centre in Sydney. It is not only committed to providing advice, referral and casework services, but also, according to its statement of objectives, sets out:

- To identify inequalities and defects in laws, the legal system, administrative practice and society which affect [the centre's] clients and disadvantaged people generally and to work for social and legal change to remove those defects and inequalities.
- To promote community legal education.
- To investigate and develop new ways of providing legal services to clients in the interests of improving access to [the centre's] services and to ensure that the quality of those services is maintained and improved.[8]

Redfern has maintained a creditable record of innovation and delivery of service. While undertaking a number of test cases and promoting a generally high media profile, it puts a premium on advice-giving and well-organised volunteer work. At any one time, it has around 40 volunteer lawyers and 80 students. In addition to daytime advice sessions, it is open five evenings a week.

Redfern has been the source of a number of new initiatives which have been developed into organisations in their own right; these include the Prisoners' Legal Service (now taken over by the commission), the Consumer Credit Legal Service, two publishing operations – Redfern Legal Centre Publishing and Streetwize Comics – and the Accommodation Rights Service. Redfern currently houses the Intellectual Disability Rights Service as a semi-independent organisation.

Specialist legal centres

Besides the organisations spawned by Redfern Legal Centre, a number of other specialist legal centres (similar to Ontario's 'specialty clinics') exist in Australia. The Consumer Credit Legal Centre (CCLC) in Victoria, established in 1982, provides exactly the kind of service advocated in chapter 5 for a specialist centre dealing with aspects of debt. Forty per cent of its funding comes from the Legal Aid Commission and most of the rest from the Ministry of Consumer Affairs, for whom it acts in the task of scrutinising applications for licences from the credit industry – the centre considers that it is better at the investigative role than the ministry.

Initially, campaigning dominated its work, and it developed a high media profile, helped by its ability to devise terms like 'sexually transmitted debt', used to describe the phenomenon of wives taking on husbands' debt.[9] More recently, the centre has moved more towards legal action. It had a spectacular test case success against a finance house, which arose out of an application for a credit licence. The centre had opposed giving the licence after handling 15 individual cases that raised problems about the company's way of dealing with borrowers. By enforcing discovery of about 7,000 documents, the centre was able to prove that the finance house was technically overcharging, and a licence was initially refused. Because not all those who had suffered financial loss could easily be traced, part of the proposed settlement involved the company's agreement to contribute towards funding a consumer law centre.

The Communications Law Centre (CLC) and the Public Interest Advocacy Centre (PIAC), both based in New South Wales, have also been involved in litigation. The CLC challenged whether ex-media magnate Alan Bond was a 'fit and proper' person to hold a broadcasting licence and has been active in supporting discussion of ownership of an important newspaper group passing into receivership. The CLC developed as an offshoot of work by PIAC in the media field and took part in challenging Kerry Packer's involvement in television. PIAC is currently addressing three major issues: toxic chemicals; motor vehicle safety, and pharmaceutical, medical and health products and services.[10] The targeting of toxic chemicals was prompted by a number of calls to the centre about the consequences of domestic pest control agents and the overnight release of toxic gases by factories; the issue of motor safety reflects the influence of US consumer campaigns, and the interest in medical products follows a strong Dalkon shield campaign.

Law foundations

Both the CLC and PIAC were set up by the Law Foundation of New South Wales. Established in 1972, the foundation has played a major role in encouraging innovation. Though based in New South Wales, its projects have made an impact throughout Australia. Funded by income from solicitors' client accounts, it is the best resourced foundation in Australia: in 1989, it distributed $3.4 million, the equivalent of 5 per cent of the Legal Aid Commission's budget. Such a sound financial base gives a tremendous boost to a range of experimental provision within the state.[11]

Besides its continuing funding commitment to the Communication Law Centre and the Public Interest Advocacy Centre, the foundation has begun another major project involving community legal centres. A preliminary report on a management support project envisages expenditure of more than $2 million over three years.

Publishing is another area that the foundation has encouraged. This is essential in a small jurisdiction in which commercial publishers are not attracted by books for relatively limited markets. Foundation money contributed to the success of Redfern Legal Centre Publishing. More recently, grants have subsidised an immigration kit, produced by the Immigration Rights Service, and a *Handbook for Social Security Advisers*, compiled by the Welfare Rights Service.

Other projects funded by the foundation include 'Courtguide', part of which involves an interactive video on court practice and procedure designed for potential litigants, and a pilot Legal Information Access Centre, based in Sydney's main library. The latter provides students (including school students, who are now all taught law at some stage in their studies) and those with no access to law libraries with written information, videos and a number of information databases. In addition to this strategic work, the foundation funds individuals to undertake small projects during study leave, often involving travel abroad.

Education and reform

Despite funding restrictions, education is seen as playing a major role in the work of legal aid commissions. It is expressly included, as we have seen, in the statutory objects of the Victoria and New South Wales Legal Aid Commissions.

The education and information division of Victoria's commission illustrates the broad scope of activities. The division deals with continuing legal education for the commission's staff, liaises with community legal centres, works with the media and provides libel services for the commission and the public. In addition, it services a staff law reform group, which feeds ideas to a joint commission-staff committee. It has a $300,000 budget for community legal education and its activities include seminars for community workers, booklets, videos aimed at non-English speakers (for example, an introduction to the legal system in three languages), a monthly advice session for non-English speakers, and DIY workshops on road traffic, divorce, child support and bankruptcy.

The commissions see legal centres as one means in which they can carry out their role in relation to community legal education. The publishing activities of some centres – for example, Redfern Legal Centre Publishing and the law foundation projects – are seen as central to community legal education.

The legal centres' commitment to education was given a clarion call in a motion adopted by a recent general meeting of Melbourne's Fitzroy Legal Centre:

- People have potential and they can develop greater power and control over their own lives.
- The Legal Service should operate as a medium of change by improving people's level of knowledge and their ability to cope, by changing laws and by raising the level of enforceability of rights.
- The Legal Service should give people access to the law.[12]

The value of community legal centre provision has been accepted by the current Australian Labour commonwealth government. In 1991, at a time when other services were under threat, it extended its commitment to centres by announcing an increase of its total resources for centres from $2.7 million to $5.2 million. The Attorney-General stated: 'It is important that mechanisms exist that will guarantee the successful development of the community legal centre movement.'[13]

References

1   The information on which this chapter is based was obtained during a visit by Roger Smith in July 1991. An exchange rate of Aus $2.34 to £1 has been assumed.

2   Interviews with officials in both commissions and the Office of Legal Aid and Family Services; Legal Aid Commission of New South Wales *Annual Report 1990*, Legal Aid Commission of Victoria *11th Statutory Report 1989/1990* and *12th Statutory Report 1990/1991*.

3   J Hartnett 'The legal aid community – working towards a common vision' in National Legal Aid Conference *Conference Proceedings, Papers and Discussions* 20–21 February 1992.

4   Quoted in National Legal Aid Advisory Committee *Legal Aid for the Australian Community* Attorney-General's Department, 1989.

5   Legal Aid Commission of Victoria *12th Statutory Report 1990/1991* p8.

6   Legal Aid Commission of Victoria *1991 Client Survey*.

7   Office of Legal Aid and Family Services, Attorney General's Department *Community Legal Centres: a study of four centres in New South Wales and Victoria* 1991, p8.

8   Redfern Legal Centre *Annual Report July 1989–June 1990*.

9   Interviews with staff at the Consumer Credit Legal Centre; Women and Credit Task Group *How to get out of sexually transmitted debt* CCLC, 1991.

10   Interviews with staff at the Communications Law Centre and the Public Interest Advocacy Centre and annual reports; *Five Years in the Ring: an account of the first five years of the Public Interest Advocacy Centre* PIAC 1987.

11 Interview with T Purcell, director, Law Foundation of New South Wales, and *1990 Annual Report.*

12 Interview with staff at Fitzroy Legal Centre, and annual reports.

13 Press release quoted in October 1991 *Legal Action 5.*

CHAPTER 11

Lessons from abroad

The development of mainstream legal services in England and Wales has been strikingly insular, except for the initial influence of the US on the law centre movement. After the second world war, a legal aid scheme was developed which was, for its time, the most comprehensive in the world. Since then, however, its form has stayed relatively untouched by the development of different approaches in other jurisdictions. Many of the proposals in Part IV of this report represent an attempt to improve the system of publicly funded legal services by absorbing lessons from other jurisdictions.

However, we should make a caveat in comparing services abroad to those in Britain. The jurisdictions studied were all very different from each other and from this country. Two – in the Netherlands and, to a lesser extent, in Quebec – are based on a less adversarial civil law system. Another very evident difference is in terms of population and geography. The population of England and Wales is just under 50 million; by comparison, the Netherlands has a population of 15 million, Ontario 9 million, Quebec 6.5 million, New South Wales 6 million and Victoria 4 million. The populations of the Canadian provinces and Australian states are scattered over vast geographical areas, while those of England and Wales are much more highly concentrated, giving rise to very different problems in meeting legal needs.

A similarity in all jurisdictions, however, is the pressure on funding. In the 1970s, spending, innovation and services expanded rapidly in an atmosphere full of energy and enthusiasm. This has now begun to evaporate – even in England and Wales, where expenditure overall actually continued to rise during the 1980s and into the 1990s. In the Netherlands and Quebec, as in England and Wales, legal aid lawyers have threatened strike action over their remuneration. Practitioners in Ontario face a government review to find savings in its certificate-based scheme. The Australian legal aid commissions face periodic funding crises. In such a widespread climate of government restraint, particular care has to be taken with, on the one hand, comparisons that might be misused and, on the other, grandiose proposals for major reform which would, if ever implemented, face chronic underfunding.

In some ways, the system of legal aid in England and Wales compares well with the other jurisdictions.[1] Net government expenditure in 1989 on legal aid represented a little under £12 per head of population. Some rudimentary indication of comparative spending can be given. New South Wales (excluding monies spent on its Aboriginal Legal Service and those channelled through its Law Foundation) and the Netherlands spent just over half of this amount, Victoria and Quebec around two-thirds and Ontario about five-sixths.

Higher expenditure in England and Wales reflects a wider scope of public legal services. For historical and cultural reasons, more public funding for legal assistance in connection with divorce is probably available in England and Wales than elsewhere. One factor certainly stands out: a higher proportion of expenditure goes on criminal work than in other jurisdictions. This is difficult to measure accurately, but some indication of the balance of criminal and civil work is given by comparing the proportion of expenditure on cases which are identified as criminal as against the cost of those identified as civil. It must, however, be stressed that these figures are not directly comparable; the ultimate balance of civil and criminal work depends on adding advice and other publicly funded legal services into the equation. It is also important to remember that no attempt has been made in this report to assess the relative quality of provision.

For England and Wales in 1990, criminal cases calculated on this basis accounted for 61 per cent of all legal aid expenditure on civil and criminal cases excluding green form advice. In Ontario, the proportion for 1989/ 90 was about the same. By contrast, the proportion in the Netherlands for 1989 was 32 per cent. In Quebec, the *Commission des Services Juridiques* apportioned casework costs as 41 per cent criminal in 1989/90. As a very rough example of the position in Australia, the New South Wales Legal Aid Commission apportioned its total cash budget in 1989/90 on the basis that about 35 per cent of its money was spent on criminal cases.

Expenditure on private practitioners dominates the legal aid budget in England and Wales: in 1991/92, the percentage of publicly funded legal services spent on law centres was just 0.3 per cent. In Ontario, the proportion spent on clinics in 1989/90 was 14 per cent of the Ontario Legal Aid Plan budget (net of administrative costs). In Quebec, the

Commission des Services Juridiques divided costs in 1989/90 between salaried and private practitioner advocates on the basis that 71 per cent of expenditure went to *commission* lawyers. Forty-two per cent of the expenditure of the New South Wales Legal Aid Commission in 1989/90 went on salaried provisions (of which 2.6 per cent went to community legal centres). In the Netherlands, 15 per cent of the legal aid budget was spent on the *buros.*

The Netherlands has the highest level of overall civil legal aid eligibility. England and Wales probably has the second highest level for matrimonial and personal injury cases. Eligibility levels in criminal cases are almost impossible to compare because of differences in the scope of matters covered; but most jurisdictions provide assistance for the equivalent of bail applications for people in custody. The existence of salaried provision, whether in the form of the *buros,* clinics, commission staff or legal centres, means that the accessibility of assistance with social welfare law problems is likely to be greater in the jurisdictions abroad.

Each jurisdiction funds law centres to some degree, though Quebec has only two, both of which are independent of the *Commission des Services Juridiques.* Commonwealth funding for Australian legal centres – already double the number of those in England and Wales for a population a third of the size – has recently been increased, while the Dutch equivalent, the *Buros voor Rechtshulp,* are a lynchpin of the whole system. In Ontario, most areas of social welfare law have been given to the community legal clinics in preference to private practitioners.

The jurisdictions that spend more money on law centres have begun to develop ways, through various forms of contracts, of seeking to combine autonomy with an element of accountability to the funding authority. The Dutch Ministry of Justice is developing a mechanism whereby *buro* funding can be sensitive to caseload. Ontario has drawn up the performance indicators reproduced in appendix 2 and introduced reporting categories, requiring its clinics to monitor not only their casework but also their community legal education and law reform activity. The Australian commonwealth government has also devised guidelines on funding (set out in appendix 2). As proposed in chapter 12, these developments should be built upon in expanding law centres in this country.

The experience of jurisdictions abroad bears out the value of a commitment to innovation. In Australia, in particular, legal centres are still experimenting with ideas about how services can best be provided and which new services should be delivered. The effectiveness of the work of the specialty clinics in Ontario and of their equivalents in Australia provides an indication of the benefits of spending a relatively small amount of money on establishing a strategic service.

Examination of other systems confirms LAG's longstanding argument that publicly funded legal services should be run by a legal aid or legal services commission. The commissions in Quebec and Australia not only administer legal aid funding but also give a direction to policy and development of services. A number of factors are required for a commission to be successful but, at least, it must have a membership independent both of government and the legal profession and a large measure of control over its own budget.

Commissions have proved that they can deliver legal services within an efficient management framework. This is particularly true of the Quebec *commission*, which has assessed the average cost and time spent on each case and has consequently been able to build in financial incentives for its salaried lawyers. The Quebec *commission* has not only proved itself an effective manager, it also holds to a perception of legal services as broader than the simple provision of advice, assistance and representation. Ontario's clinics, Quebec's *commission* and the Australian legal aid commissions have all shown that education and law reform are also an important part of public legal provision.

This view is reflected in Part IV, which lays out LAG's proposals for the future of publicly funded legal services in England and Wales.

References

1 In making comparisons, all figures given are for 1989 or 1989/90. More recent statistics are available for some jurisdictions.

Part IV

Equal access to justice

CHAPTER 12

The scope of legal services

Legal aid in England and Wales remains dominated by the narrow framework in which it was originally conceived. Other jurisdictions, as we have seen, have developed a broader view. For instance, in the Australian state of Victoria, legal aid has been statutorily defined to mean not only 'any legal services that may be provided by a legal practitioner', but also 'education, advice and information in and about the law' and a range of other legal services specified in the legislation.[1] LAG argues for a similarly wide view of legal services in this country. The traditional concept of providing advice, assistance and representation should be seen as only one element in publicly funded legal services. Along with the broadening of the definition, there is a need for greater planning in how those services are delivered.

The role of legal services

The unifying theme in legal services policy must be the acceptance of an overall objective against which success or failure can be measured. For LAG, that objective is the attainment of equal access to justice for all members of society. This firmly shifts the emphasis from the means by which publicly funded legal services are delivered to their intended result.

The addition of 'equal' to the usual 'access to justice' phrase is deliberate. The promotion of access to justice is now almost a cliché. The basic approach encouraged by its early academic promoters was to place legal services in the context of 'the full panoply of institutions, procedures and persons that characterise our judicial system'.[2] People excluded from justice not only need accessible lawyers but also accessible procedures, adjudication and laws. Even the early proselytisers saw the potential problems: 'The risk is that the use of rapid procedures and inexpensive   111 personnel will produce cheap and unrefined products. This risk must be kept continually in mind.'[3]

The risk was real. The language of 'access to justice' has been eagerly taken up by governments wishing to save money on publicly funded legal services. For instance, the final report of the Civil Justice Review in 1988 contained a chapter entitled 'Access to Justice', but made only one general recommendation about legal aid: 'As a matter of priority the Legal Aid Board should take early action to reduce the time taken to handle applications for civil legal aid.'[4] Yet its main proposal was for greater devolution of cases throughout the court system from High to county court and from the county court to the small claims procedure. Such moves have profound legal aid implications. The report omitted to consider, or even mention, the consequence that legal aid would no longer be available for those cases deemed suitable for transfer to the small claims procedure. Only subsequently was there any recognition that personal injury cases can pose severe difficulties, as shown in chapter 4, for litigants without representation.

The ultimate policy aim must be that anyone with a legal problem has equal access to its just conclusion so that disputes are determined by the intrinsic merits of the arguments of either party, not by inequalities of wealth or power. To achieve this, legal aid policy alone provides too narrow a focus. It is necessary to consider a more comprehensive range of policies relating to the totality of publicly funded legal services. We have called this the 'legal services approach'.

The legal services approach provides three means by which equal access to justice may be attained. In addition to the provision of advice, assistance and representation (defined as the statutory goals of legal aid in the Legal Aid Act 1988), it stresses the importance of both education and information and the reform of law and procedure.

For 20 years, LAG has been critical of the lack of strategic planning in relation to legal services. In its evidence to the Royal Commission on Legal Services in 1977, the Group repeated its concern that 'there is no national policy for the provision of publicly financed legal services'.[5] This remains the case today. Legal aid rates of eligibility and remuneration are, it is true, set nationally. However, their levels lack any logic and the actual provision of services is determined by the vagaries of market forces on individual practitioners. Similarly, the distribution of law centres and advice agencies is independent of any national assessment of need, depending instead on the varying attitudes and financial health of local authorities.

Chapter 13 discusses the consequences of a legal services approach in terms of administration and organisation. Chapter 14 deals with these implications in terms of how legal services should be delivered. Here, we consider the principles that should underlie the provision of all publicly funded legal services.

Education and information

Equal access to justice requires all members of society to be aware of their rights and obligations. Acceptance of an educational role for publicly funded legal services is closely linked to the currently fashionable idea of 'citizenship'. The British are, in law, more subjects of the Crown than citizens of the country. British citizenship is so legally insubstantial that it does not even give an automatic right of residence. What is required is a fundamental transformation in the status of all members of British society, whereby they will be able to exercise real rights.

Vital to this process is knowledge of the law. This is as true in relation to general provisions of the law as it is to the consumer rights which have been the focus of a range of current citizenship initiatives.

The need for information in relation to the rights and obligations of citizens has been stressed by many commentators. The Speaker's Commission on Citizenship recommended 'a review and codification of the law relating to legal rights, duties and entitlements of the citizen in the United Kingdom and the dissemination of this information in a clear way to all citizens', and urged 'the Lord Chancellor to invite the government and other appropriate individuals and institutions to consult on the best way of ensuring these objectives'.[6]

The government's commitment to citizenship carries a similar emphasis: 'openness', 'information' and 'accessibility' are key elements of the 'principles of public service' in its Citizen's Charter.[7] These are as relevant for legal services as for public services; indeed, much of the government's description of basic principle is directly transferable. For instance, just as 'full, accurate information should be readily available, in plain language' on the public services that the citizen may choose to use, so it should be on the law that imposes on a citizen.

The Legal Aid Board and, before it, the Law Society have accepted responsibility for some measure of information about legal aid. The Legal Aid Act 1988 gives the board specific power 'to promote or assist in the promotion of publicity'.[8] Although the board has produced a very good range of leaflets and forms, its commitment to advertising has, over time, been uneven. In fact, it was recently criticised for its lack of adequate publicity in a National Audit Office report (see p27). The statutory power should be converted into a positive duty to inform those likely to be eligible of the services available to them. Furthermore, the effectiveness with which this duty is carried out should be monitored by annual surveys of the target population.

The adoption of a legal services approach entails, however, a much wider commitment to education and information than simply more advertising for legal aid. Such a commitment can be seen in the examples of education work undertaken by the *Commission des Services Juridiques* in Quebec and the Australian legal aid commissions. Furthermore, the Office of Fair Trading, with a range of clear and attractive material on the subject of consumer rights, provides a domestic example of what can be done. There needs to be an institution which takes on a similar role in relation to the rights of citizens more generally, a function widely known abroad as 'public legal education'. Such a responsibility might extend as far as encouraging legal education in school. Some work in this field has already been done: the Law Society established an imaginative 'Law in schools' project which has now been taken over by the Citizenship Foundation. The Legal Aid Board is ideally placed to take on this public legal education function.

This sort of initiative ought to be encouraged if a commitment to citizenship by government is to have any real meaning. The very act of establishing a national body with an express responsibility for legal education and awareness would be a catalyst to further development. Such a project could have a considerable effect without a very large budget. Developments like the 'Courtguide' programme in New South Wales (see p101) even offer the potential to save money, at least in terms of court and tribunal staff time. Using interactive technology – whereby a clip of film can be shown as the answer to a question – it is possible to guide people undertaking their own cases through courts and tribunals.

Within a legal services approach, education can also provide an alternative method of dealing with people's problems. Some of the Australian legal aid commissions, for instance, provide classes for women going through divorce or seeking child support, deliberately substituting a 'do-it-yourself' approach within an educational framework for traditional lawyer-client casework. Some clients might actually prefer this alternative, as it may be a less isolating experience. The same might be true for those seeking advice on debt. With money saved in legal aid costs, such classes could be offered to all on a non-fee paying basis.

Another example is already provided by law centres. They, and their equivalents in other jurisdictions, have developed a variety of imaginative educational approaches in order to help people facing a common problem work towards a common solution. This is often known as community action or community work. It is, however, perhaps best described by the phrase 'community legal education'.

Law reform

Law reform, to a British observer, may not seem an immediately obvious aim for publicly funded legal services. It is, in fact, crucial for the following reasons.

First, a legal services approach requires consideration of what services are to be provided within the context of the reform of law and procedure. The divorce reforms proposed in 1976, which removed the need for court hearings in undefended divorces and thereby shifted the balance of legal aid expenditure (see p36), stand as a model of what can be done. In contrast, an integrated consideration of legal procedure and legal aid was lacking from the Civil Justice Review, the Legal Aid Board's multi-party action proposals and the Lord Chancellor's Department suggestion for a 'safety net' system for civil legal aid. Compartmentalising discussions on legal aid and on court procedures does not allow for the development of coherent, integrated policies.

Mechanisms must be developed whereby proposals to reform law and procedure are accompanied by a consideration of the likely effects – either negative or positive: what legal services will need to be provided and what their cost will be. In Australia, for instance, proposed commonwealth legislation is accompanied by a 'legal aid impact statement' to encourage this approach. Such a requirement should be introduced in this country.

Second, it must be recognised that traditional forms of litigation taken by individuals are not always the best way of handling disputes. There are various alternatives: some cases can be removed from the courts and resolved by alternative means, such as by tribunals or through conciliation; certain disputes require the development of collective procedures, such as multi-party personal injury litigation, and some rights may be better enforced through third parties, such as the Health and Safety Executive or the Commission for Racial Equality.

Third, it follows that the Legal Aid Board, or any future administrator of publicly funded legal services, should play a much larger role in promoting the links between legal services, substantive law and procedure. The board cannot function properly within a remit confined to legal aid. Its limited approach to multi-party actions made this very apparent. Yet, the problems in the Opren case illustrate just how much these issues of law and procedure need tackling.

The board should both initiate, and respond to, proposals for law reform – for instance, by making published submissions to suggestions for reform from the Law Commission. This would introduce the legal services approach into public debate. Current concern about the overall level of legal aid expenditure, which is largely determined by the cost of criminal cases, provides an example of what is required. A narrow approach to this problem has led the government to advocate fixed fees for solicitors in magistrates' courts, to keep down unit costs. This may curtail the rise in expenditure, but the effect is likely to be relatively marginal. A proper solution requires consideration of whether so many cases need to be brought before the court in the first place, and whether magistrates need such extensive powers of imprisonment. Either or both might allow savings to the legal aid budget, but they require a far more integrated approach to reform than seems possible under the present circumstances.

Fourth, the contribution that experienced legal aid practitioners could make to law reform should be recognised. The remit of publicly funded legal services should include an aim similar to that of the CAB service: to 'exercise a responsible influence on the development of social policies and services, both locally and nationally'. This role for the CABx was explicitly accepted by a government-sponsored review in 1984: 'Not only do we think that such exercises are proper and useful, but that the CAB Service would be open to criticism if it did not undertake them.'[9]

The Legal Aid Board should foster ways in which the practitioners it funds could contribute, as legal aid providers rather than Law Society members, to responsible policy discussion. An obvious method would be to fund groups of practitioners in particular fields, such as criminal defence, so that they could put forward distinctive views on how the system of justice might be improved. The next chapter suggests that, in furtherance of this approach, the board should take over the functions of the Lord Chancellor's Advisory Committee of Legal Aid, as a stimulator of debate within and outside government.

Advice, assistance and representation

It is fundamental to a legal services approach that legal aid should be seen as only one component in a broad range of provision. A comprehensive view of legal services must include all legal advice, assistance and representation, ranging from preliminary advice with a legal component provided by agencies like the CABx to the specialised advocacy services of Queen's Counsel. A more integrated approach, where such functions are not looked at, or funded, completely separately, is essential to LAG's model of how publicly funded legal services should be delivered.

Furthermore, the definition of representation needs to be expanded. Legal aid has been dominated by the need for services related to litigation. A committee of the Canadian Bar Association showed itself open to a broader approach: '"Legal services" need not be narrowed to standard litigation orientated services. For the private client, the lawyer offers the full range of advocacy on behalf of his or her client, not just individual representation before the courts, but also preventive legal advice, non-adversarial representation, representation before tribunals, client legal education, formal and informal efforts to change laws affecting clients. If legal aid plans have an avowed goal of providing equal access to legal services for their clients, then they too should obtain the benefit of the full range of a lawyer's services, constrained only by the demands of the client's case.'[10]

Publicly funded legal services must be made accessible to those that need them. The Legal Aid Board must be responsible for planning where and how services are to be delivered. There must also be a coherent policy in relation to eligibility, constructed upon a set of clearly expressed principles. In LAG's view, the form of provision should reflect several important considerations.

First, there should be a tier of publicly funded legal services to provide immediate diagnostic advice and information. This should be free to any enquirer and highly accessible. The traditional perception of this frontline function as separate from 'proper' legal services is unhelpful. The need for such general advice services must be recognised as national; though how that need is met may vary around the country. Advice agencies may continue to have other functions, but their basic role is to be an information and referrral point on which much of the edifice of publicly funded legal services is based.

Second, some areas of legal need should be given priority and assistance with them should be free of charge, regardless of means. LAG has long argued that some services must be regarded as essential and delivered on this basis, though tests of sufficient merit may be retained. In 1986, we listed these as including services that deal with 'disputes over residential accommodation, settlement of disputes about custody of children, compensation of those suffering bodily injury, protection of persons in fear of attack and assault, protection against dismissal or exclusion from employment or occupation, defence of persons accused of any crime punishable by imprisonment, protection against wrongful imprisonment, and protection of rights of entry and residence in the United Kingdom'.

The government has made some recent moves towards its own prioritisation: legal aid is available without a means test in relation to certain disputes about children, and advice in the police station is also seen as sufficiently important to be given without charge.

LAG stands by its concept of 'essential legal services' meriting free provision, though recognising both that attainment of this is a long-term goal and that, in practice, the detail of the list of essential services is open to discussion.

Third, greater priority must be given to the field of social welfare law, including providing representation at tribunals. At present, legal services in this area are inadequate. A number of the matters in LAG's list of essential services relate to landlord and tenant, immigration and employment law. Immigration and employment are also areas of law in which the lack of tribunal repesentation clearly puts people at a disadvantage. Representation by specialists in the relevant area of law and procedure – who may not themselves need to be qualified lawyers, but should have easy access to them – must be made available.

Legal aid, as currently conceived, is not well suited to deliver such a service. For instance, as we saw in chapter 6, the statutory charge is generally inappropriate in tribunal proceedings: costs are not usually available from the losing side in tribunal cases, so that the expense cannot be offset in the same way as is possible in court-based litigation. In any event, expertise in social welfare law has been fostered by law centres and advice agencies, and should be built upon. Such bodies already deliver free services. Clients in landlord and tenant cases, employment, immigration, debt and social security cases are, on the whole, sufficiently likely to be poor as to merit the withdrawal of an individual means test (relatively wealthy people with problems in these areas are likely to consult private solicitors). Financial eligibility can, therefore, be defined by subject matter rather than by the means of individual clients.

Eligibility

The question of financial eligibility levels, where relevant, must be worked out on a sensible basis. A prerequisite for this is that legal services should, insofar as possible, be provided through one integrated system. LAG argued in 1982 that 'the green form and civil legal aid schemes should be unified on the basis of one assessment of the applicant's means done by the solicitor at the beginning of the case. The financial criteria should function like those used for the present green form scheme, but with allowances for actual rents, rates and mortgage payments.'[11] LAG continues to advocate this position, with the proviso that eligibility levels should be determined on the bases outlined below. It may also be that some problematic cases of eligibility – involving, for instance, self-employed people – should continue to be determined by a central administration.

Legal aid should, therefore, be simplified so that an applicant faces only one eligibility test at the beginning of a case. This would not prevent the grant of subsidised legal services being approved in stages by the appropriate authority, nor the imposition of further contributions at different points of a case – for instance, to cover advice and then representation. But there is a clear distinction between this situation and the government's proposal, whereby legal aid contributions, which may be completely arbitrary and out of the control of the contributor, would be payable throughout the duration of a case. If contributions are to be charged, they must be based on clear principles which are explained at the outset of a case so that clients know and can measure the extent of their liability. These principles should include the following:

a) A relatively high proportion of the population must be financially eligible. To ensure consistency, income and capital limits should be linked to changes in the level of average earnings or income support. The Lord Chancellor's Advisory Committee on Legal Aid, in its 27th report, recommended that the lower income limit for free civil legal aid and dependants' additions should be set at 50 per cent above what would now be income support levels.[12] This represents the sort of benchmark LAG would propose. Capital limits should also be raised to an equivalent level above those applicable for income support.

The upper limit for any means test should be sufficiently high to allow for all those who would otherwise be unable, for financial reasons, to consider taking or defending legal proceedings. There should be an element of discretion so that limits can be raised for particularly expensive types of case, such as medical negligence litigation, which are otherwise outside the reach even of people with relatively high incomes and capital. Contributions could be set above a reasonable upper limit at 100 per cent of legal aid costs. The advantage to clients would be access to lawyers acting on legal aid rates and subject to legal aid quality control, as well as some element of protection against an order for costs if a case is lost.

b) Financial eligibility should also be extended wherever this can be done, at little or no cost. In matrimonial and personal injury cases, the large bulk of civil legally aided work, it could be extended without much additional expense. The existence of the statutory charge would offset much of the cost in relation to matrimonial cases. Similarly, the indemnity costs rule leads to a recoupment of legal aid expenditure in a high proportion of personal injury cases. As the Lord Chancellor's working party on financial eligibility declined to give figures for the cost of extending eligibility in this way, the appropriate research should be commissioned or a closely monitored experiment undertaken to see what the potential costs would be.

c) Contributions must be set at reasonable levels. The percentage of income over the minimum eligibility level which is taken as a contribution should be reduced from one-quarter to one-fifth.

d) Particular considerations must apply to legal aid in criminal cases. Contributions in such cases, introduced by the Legal Aid Act 1982, have never recovered the sums hoped for by the Lord Chancellor's Department and, at £3.4 million in 1991/92,[13] probably do not cover their full collection costs. It is, in any event, clearly unjust to charge criminal defendants for the costs of their defence unless, and until, they are found guilty. Even then, it must be recognised that legal aid contributions will have a lower priority than either fines or compensation and will remain largely irrelevant as a source of additional revenue.

LAG's view is that legal representation should be given free to defendants accused of any offence carrying the possibility of imprisonment. This cannot be reduced to any pre-judgment, either by the court or an outside body, on the likelihood of imprisonment under the differing sentencing policies of particular courts. Furthermore, the mechanism for reducing expenditure on criminal legal aid – if this is considered necessary – is clear: reduce the range of minor offences that can incur imprisonment.

These considerations aside, courts have an interest in high levels of representation. The administration of many magistrates' courts, particularly those with lay benches, would collapse if there was any significant withdrawal of legal aid – as might be the case if draconian rules about proof of income were re-introduced. As for the Crown Court, its operation would become completely impossible if large numbers of defendants were forced to represent themselves.

Similar steps should be taken for the integration of the differing systems of advice and assistance as proposed above for civil legal aid above. However, some form of duty solicitor scheme which is effective, free and non-means tested must immediately be available to persons in custody prior to determination of their case by a court.

Certain improvements must be made urgently, without prejudice to other developments. For instance, publicly funded representation should be extended to the coroner's courts, where hearings have become significantly more contentious in recent years. This has been particularly evident in 'disaster' cases such as the Hillsborough deaths, where families of the bereaved had to pay privately for representation, and in deaths in custody, where the bereaved often have to rely on the help of the organisation, Inquest, or on the chance of getting the services of a barrister free of charge. Representation might be provided either through some extension of ABWOR or by funding a central agency, as advocated by Inquest.

Some form of representation must also be extended to those tribunals which are concerned with substantive points of law or crucially affect the rights of the citizen. This could most easily be effected by an extension of ABWOR. In particular, representation should be automatically available for hearings before the social security commissioners. In such cases, an appeal is only possible with leave; it must be on a point of law, and the matter at issue usually relates to some basic social security benefit. A similarly strong case can be made for hearings before the immigration appeal tribunal. This is an appellate body rehearing cases decided at first instance; appeal requires leave, and its decisions can lead to exclusion from the country. In both these situations, the individual's claim is being contested by what is effectively a government department. That department is always represented by a skilled lay advocate and often by a lawyer. Lack of representation in such cases is clearly a denial of equal access to justice.

References

1   s2 Legal Aid Commission Act 1981 (Vic).
2   M Cappelletti and B Garth *Access to Justice: a world survey* Sitjoff and Noordhoff, 1978, Vol 1, p49.

3   As in 2 above, p124.

4   Civil Justice Review *Report of the Review Body on Civil Justice* Cm 394, HMSO, 1988, recommendation 56, p159.

5   Legal Action Group *Legal Services: a blueprint for the future* LAG, 1977, p4.

6   Commission on Citizenship *Encouraging Citizenship* HMSO, 1990, recommendation 10, pxix.

7   *Citizen's Charter* HMSO, 1991, p5.

8   s4(2)(e) Legal Aid Act 1988.

9   *Review of the National Association of Citizens Advice Bureaux* (the 'Lovelock report'), 1984, Cmnd 9139, para 6.3.

10 National Legal Aid Liaison Committee of the Canadian Bar Association *Legal Aid Delivery Models: a discussion paper* 1987, p181.

11 Legal Action Group *Submission on the Financial Criteria for the Grant of Legal Aid to the Legal Aid Advisory Committee Review of Legal Aid* LAG, 1983.

12 Lord Chancellor's Office *27th Legal Aid Annual Reports* [1976–77] HC 172, HMSO, 1978, p120.

13 *HC Hansard written answers* 1 July 1992, cols 575–6.

Administration of legal services

The administration of publicly funded legal services must be reorganised in the light of the strategic approach advocated in the previous chapter. An indication of the failure of the current arrangements is given by the growth of legal aid expenditure at consistently higher rates than foreseen by the Lord Chancellor's Department. As shown in chapter 2, departmental estimates published in February 1991 predicted that net legal aid expenditure for 1991/92 would total £698 million; a year later, its estimated outturn was £907 million,[1] far beyond the usual margin of error that is acceptable in the battle of wits between a spending department and the Treasury.

The continuing disparity between estimated and actual expenditure is undoubtedly one of the major factors in causing the Treasury to demand savings from the Lord Chancellor's Department budget with increased force. A series of measures, of which the imposition of fixed fees for a wider range of legal aid cases is but one, can be expected as the department fights to get its costs under control. The overrun on expenditure is, however, indicative of a problem which no amount of hasty cuts will solve: the mechanisms by which policy is developed, services planned and costs controlled are inadequate.

Legal aid administration was reformed after the 1986 efficiency scrutiny recommended its transfer from the Law Society to a government-appointed board. The proposals first contained in the March 1987 white paper, *Legal Aid in England and Wales: a new framework*,[2] and ultimately implemented in the Legal Aid Act 1988, never went far enough. The white paper expressly stated that the new board would initially 'do no more than take over those functions performed by the Law Society'. Suggested further roles to be transferred at a later date – such as the 'assessment of means, decisions of the grant of criminal legal aid, and at least some of the determination of bills now carried out in the courts' – were simply matters of 'good housekeeping'.

123

The Legal Aid Board has improved the administration which it inherited, but it is now time to take a more fundamental look at the organisation of legal aid and publicly funded legal services. This involves detailed examination of the functions of the following:

- the government
- the Legal Aid Board
- the legal aid advisory committee
- regional legal services committees.

Only in the context of reform of these four elements in legal service provision can sensible long-term strategies be evolved on policy priorities.

The government

Lord Mackay addressed the question of possible change to the office of Lord Chancellor in his 1991 inaugural Mishcon lecture. He concluded that the office 'provides a link, which our long history of gradual development has produced, between the judiciary, the executive and the legislature which is broken at our peril'.[3]

His lecture began with an authoritative description of the 'three most important features of the modern post – judge, minister and parliamentarian'. As judge, the Lord Chancellor is head of the judiciary, presiding chair of the Appellate Committee of the House of Lords and the Judicial Committee of the Privy Council, president of the Supreme Court, president of the Chancery Division of the High Court and the 'controlling authority' of the county courts. These titles are not entirely honorary. Lord Mackay sat as a judge 13 times in the three and a half years between his appointment in October 1987 and March 1991.

The Lord Chancellor is also a member of the cabinet responsible for judicial appointments and the administration of justice. Much debate about the post of Lord Chancellor has focused on the potential problem of a member of the executive appointing the judiciary. In fact, a more practical difficulty arises from combining political responsibility for aspects of legal affairs with judicial functions. The post of Lord Chancellor has only been sustained in its present form because, until recently, the executive functions of the office could be exercised in a relatively non-partisan way. This is no longer the case.

Senior members of the judiciary have already been stung into open opposition by Lord Mackay's proposals for reform of the Bar's monopoly on the rights of audience in the higher courts. Legal aid may become another politically controversial area if the government decides seriously to curb the growth in expenditure. Cuts have hitherto been marginal. They have also been mitigated by the sort of cross-party gesture that saw Conservative Lords Hailsham and Mackay continue to support the law centres first bailed out by Lord Elwyn Jones, their Labour predecessor, despite their express policy that law centre funding was a local, not a central, government responsibility. A serious attempt to bring down the rising level of expenditure is, however, bound to involve politically controversial decisions.

Some recognition of the tensions in the role has been shown by the government's appointment of a parliamentary secretary to the Lord Chancellor in the House of Commons, giving members of parliament the opportunity to debate public expenditure with a relevant minister present. That post is likely to grow in responsibility as MPs demand increasing accountability for the actions and policies of the Lord Chancellor's Department.

The Lord Chancellor's Department should become directly responsible to a minister in the House of Commons. Its responsibilities, already split between two disparate functions, should be formally separated. Legal aid policy has suffered from the precedence given to professional matters, such as the appointment of the judiciary and Queen's Counsel. This has impeded the development of sensible policy, as instanced by the Legal Aid Board's rejection of the 'safety net' approach to civil legal aid (see p12). It has also encouraged too 'ad hoc' an approach to policy, rather than the making of hard political choices, as instanced by the lack of a coherent strategy in the face of the rising costs of the legal aid budget. The danger in this approach is that, in the longer term, any cutbacks may be more drastic and piecemeal than if they had been planned for over a number of years.

As a first step, the parliamentary secretary should assume responsibility for the administration of the courts and legal aid within the Lord Chancellor's Department. In the longer term, the Lord Chancellor's power to appoint judges should be transferred to a judicial commission. The department should then be divided between that commission and a new ministry. The Lord Chancellor would remain the most senior member of the judiciary, accorded special status as speaker of the House of Lords.

Irrespective of this proposal, responsibility for legal aid and general advice agencies should be brought within one department so that an integrated network of provision can be developed. This requires, under present departmental responsibilities, the Lord Chancellor's Department to take over the current role of the Department of Trade and Industry, which provides about £10 million a year core funding for the National Association of Citizens Advice Bureaux as well as certain project funds for the Federation of Independent Advice Centres.

The DTI role dates from 1975, when the Department of Prices and Consumer Protection (now subsumed within the DTI) took over 'a sponsorship role' in relation to NACAB. The continuing responsibility has already been officially questioned: the 1984 Lovelock review of the CAB service reported that 'the logic of the link between the two is not as obvious today as it was'.[4] It pointed out that a relatively small percentage of CABx enquiries actually related to the responsibilities of the DTI, but continued, 'given the importance of the principle of independence to the service, there might also be advantage in retaining as sponsor a department where prime responsibilities lie outside the social sector'. It concluded that it held 'no strong views on the matter'. However, the review considered only what was then the Department of Health and Social Security as an alternative, not the Lord Chancellor's Department.

The advice sector, as a whole, benefits from the element of diversity introduced by the Federation of Independent Advice Centres (FIAC), which represents a much looser and diverse coalition of agencies than NACAB envisages for the CAB service. The work of these independent advice agencies should be encouraged. They can, for instance, represent more specific groups and communities, and some of them have developed a greater involvement in counselling than would be possible for the CAB service. National core funding to support its work should, therefore, be available to FIAC if it wished to accept it.

There is a tension between the need for some nationally determined level of provision and the traditional acceptance of local funding. The advice agencies themselves, through the Advice Services Alliance, have sought to accommodate these two positions by arguing for a statutory duty on local authorities to fund sufficient agencies to meet the advice needs in their area. In support of such an argument, there have been attempts to establish figures for minimum advice needs per head of population.

The form of local advice provision should remain the responsibility of local government. To this end, local authorities should be required by statute to examine the advice needs within their area and to publish proposals for meeting them. A minimum level of provision should be assured by some form of grant-aid from central government. The Legal

Aid Board should advise on satisfactory provision and encourage experimentation and the development of national standards and policies.

Towards a legal services commission

The development of a legal services approach requires reform of the Legal Aid Board in three ways: change of statutory functions, change of membership and change of name.

The current statutory framework is set out in the Legal Aid Act 1988. This created the Legal Aid Board, but did little more than transfer to it the existing powers of the Law Society. The limited nature of the Legal Aid Board's remit can be seen by a comparison with the functions given to the legal aid commissions in Australia (see p94) and Quebec's *Commission des Services Juridiques* (see p89). A model for a body with a similarly wide remit in a British context was suggested by the Scottish Royal Commission on Legal Services in 1980. It proposed something close to the sort of legal services approach advocated in this report, though lacking the concern with law reform that LAG would stress, to be implemented by an administrative institution with the following functions: 'the provision of public information as to legal rights and services . . . developing lay advice and representation at tribunals and training for lay representatives . . . studying and experimenting with the best use of law centres . . . grants to advice centres and law centres, the conduct of research, experimenting with ways to provide services, and the setting of standards . . . providing financial assistance to firms of solicitors to establish themselves in underprovided areas . . . administering legal aid . . . developing money management counselling . . . publishing advice on how to leave one's affairs in good order.'⁵

The functions of the Legal Aid Board, which has now had time to absorb the Law Society's administrative role, should be expanded in line with the legal services approach outlined in the previous chapter. Its principle objective should be 'to ensure equal access to justice'. This requires the board:

- to ensure the provision of advice, assistance and representation of a quality that every member of society has equal access to justice;
- to initiate and carry out educational programmes designed to promote an understanding by the public, or by sections of the public, of their rights, powers, privileges and duties under the law (derived from the New South Wales Legal Aid Commission Act 1979);
- to monitor, particularly in those areas most relevant to those who are

the clients of publicly funded legal services, the effect of the law and the legal system upon the community or sections of it as individuals and to initiate or respond to proposals for law reform (derived from the mission statement of the Victoria Legal Aid Commission);
- to undertake research into all aspects of legal aid including investigation and assessment of different methods of financing and providing publicly funded legal service (derived from the New South Wales Legal Aid Commission Act 1979).

The Legal Aid Board, under the provisions of the Legal Aid Act 1988, must have a membership of between 11 and 17. Two members must be solicitors appointed after consultation with the Law Society. As for barristers, the rather cryptic instruction is that 'the Lord Chancellor shall consult the General Council of the Bar with a view to the inclusion on the Board of at least two'. Otherwise, the Lord Chancellor's power of appointment is unrestricted except for the need to 'have regard to the desirability of securing that the Board includes persons having an expertise or knowledge of:
a) the provision of legal services;
b) the work of the courts and social conditions; and
c) management.'

Lord Mackay has paid particular attention to the last point: six out of 12 of the original members of the board had experience of management, but little of legal services or the courts; today, the figure is even higher.

Such an emphasis on business experience may have been justified by the board's initial task of improving the ramshackle administration bequeathed by the Law Society, but circumstances have now changed. Even if its remit is not extended, the board's membership should gradually be altered to reflect more practical experience of the services for which it is responsible and more concern with the formulation of legal services policy. A reasonable balance might be to aim at replacing half of the current members from business backgrounds with people who have practical experience of legal services, as the existing members' contracts come up for renewal.

If the board is to adopt a wider legal services role, altering the balance of its membership is not enough. Its independence must also be guaranteed. LAG proposes a membership of 12 composed as follows:

a) Five members on the basis of their 'expertise in or knowledge of the provision of legal services, education, the work of the courts and social conditions or management'. No more than three would, however, be appointed on the basis of management experience or knowledge alone. At least two should have some knowledge of education.

b) Seven members based on nominations made from a range of bodies representing consumers and providers of publicly funded legal services.

The Legal Aid Board would no longer be an appropriate title for the body envisaged by LAG. It should be renamed the Legal Services Commission.

Such plans would take time to develop. In the meantime, two innovations, both drawing from the Australian experience, should be introduced. First, the board should undertake and publish two surveys as part of its annual report, one giving a basic profile of clients assisted and the other, as recommended in the previous chapter, on the extent of knowledge about publicly funded legal services, along the lines of the survey carried out by the board in 1990.[6] These would help to shift the focus from those who deliver services to those who receive them.

Second, the board should hold a biennial conference to discuss the provision of publicly funded legal services. The agenda of a similar conference, organised by the Australian equivalent of the Lord Chancellor's Department in 1992, shows how the legal services debate can be given a much wider context than would be expected from such an event in this country. The first day alone contained workshop sessions on the following subjects: locational disadvantage, cultural disadvantage, practices and procedures, people with special needs, restrictive practices and economic restraints, community legal education, paralegals, pro bono work by lawyers, alternative funding schemes, alternative dispute resolution and jurisdictional reform.[7]

The legal aid advisory committee

The Lord Chancellor's Advisory Committee on Legal Aid originated as a public check on the operation of the Law Society in administering public funds which were paid largely to its own members. It flourished in the late 1970s, with a strong membership and its own consultant appointed from outside the civil service, providing independent criticism and policy contributions. With the transfer of legal aid administration to the Legal Aid Board, its future became unclear; it produced its 39th annual report covering 1988/89 and was then effectively disbanded for a time.

In 1991, it was reconstituted with a new membership. But section 35 of the Legal Aid Act 1988 – which states that the committee 'shall continue in being' but may be dissolved in the future – betrays the government's grudging approach. The committee's function is to advise 'on such questions relating to the provision of advice, assistance and representation under this Act as [the Lord Chancellor] shall refer to them [sic] and to make recommendations or furnish comments to him on such matters as they consider appropriate'. However, its renewed role 'will concentrate on organising conferences at which publicly funded legal services will be discussed'.[8] The committee must still report annually to parliament, but the Lord Chancellor does not have to refer the Legal Aid Board's annual report to it for comment, as he was obliged to do when the Law Society was in charge of legal aid administration.

The need for wide-ranging discussion and in-depth scrutiny of legal aid services is as necessary as ever. But the existence of the committee – which is in danger of being dismissed as a 'talking shop' – operates both to marginalise such activity and to inhibit the board from undertaking a central role in bringing debate on future policy to prominence. The committee, therefore, should be dissolved and its functions performed by the board itself, as part of its wider brief.

Regional legal services committees

The final element in the administration of legal services should be the institution of regional legal services committees. Three such committees – for Manchester, Cumbria and Lancashire – are currently in operation, forming a confederation as the North Western Legal Services Committee, with a combined executive committee and a shared secretariat. Initially started by the Law Society in 1976, the North Western Legal Services Committee has been one of the continuing successes of the legal services movement of the 1970s. It has combined a wide membership of practising solicitors, probation officers, lay advisers, social workers and others and, on very limited resources, has delivered an array of new projects. Two examples of its work are its current survey of facilities in local courts and its involvement in producing leaflets for clients and referral agencies on what to expect from a solicitor.

A further indication of the work such committees can undertake comes from the broad objects of the North Western committee. These are:

to monitor, co-ordinate and improve legal services in the North West of England, and to make legal services more widely available and accessible, and in particular to:

(i) identify the legal services in the North West, and to assess their effectiveness

(ii) assess the need for legal services in the North West and pin-point unmet need

(iii) co-ordinate the work of the various local agencies providing legal services

(iv) stimulate improvements in legal services

(v) promote legal services which do not exist in the North West

(vi) keep the public informed as to the availability of legal services

(vii) provide training on legal matters and information to any group or individual who is in need of it

(viii) liaise with professional bodies whose activities may enhance the work of the Committee.

The north-west regional committees have had great success in their additional role of disseminating information on the need for legal services and on innovative ways of providing them, sparking a national debate.

Regional legal services committees are an experiment which has been shown to work. The cost of the three in the north west is currently met by the Legal Aid Board. Attempts to establish similar committees in South Wales and the north east have floundered because of the lack of resources. The necessary funds are, in fact, likely to be very modest. The example of the north west shows how much goodwill can be drawn upon if sufficient money is put into central liaison. A gradual process should be commenced of fostering the establishment of regional legal services committees with modest secretariats – for instance, two people, as in the north west – and a modest budget for overheads, assistance in defraying travel costs of committee members, and a small amount for project work. Costs can be kept low by locating the secretariat in the area offices of the Legal Aid Board.

At a local level, the regional legal services committees in the north west have carried out the kind of innovative work and played the sort of co-ordinating role which we would expect to see from a legal services commission at a national level. The Legal Aid Board could develop such committees as part of its regional structure, thus re-orientating itself towards greater contact with practitioners in a wide range of agencies. This is particularly important if there is to be more experimentation with how services are to be delivered, as the next chapter advocates.

References

1 *The Government's Expenditure Plans 1991–92 to 1993–94* Cm 1510, HMSO, 1991, p1 and *The Government's Expenditure Plans 1992–93 to 1994–95* Cm 1910, HMSO, p1.

2   Cm 118, HMSO, 1987.
3   Speech, 6 March 1991.
4   *Review of the National Association of Citizens Advice Bureaux* Cmnd 39, HMSO, 1984, p80.
5   Royal Commission on Legal Services in Scotland *Report* Cmnd 7846, HMSO, 1980, Volume 1, para 20.10.
6   National Audit Office *The Administration of Legal Aid in England and Wales* HC 90, HMSO, 1992, para 6.5.
7   National Legal Aid Conference *Legal Aid; Legal Access: conference papers*, University of Sydney, 20–21 February 1992.
8   Lord Chancellor's Department press release, 17 July 1991.

CHAPTER 14

Delivery of legal services

A comprehensive and coherent system of delivering publicly funded legal services must fulfil a number of criteria: it must ensure services of an appropriate quality; the services must be accessible, and it must provide the best means of delivery for each particular area of work.

The beginnings of a broader approach to provision than has previously been accepted in this country are perhaps hinted at in the 1990/91 annual report of the Legal Aid Board. In this, the board provides a definition of 'access to legal services' that echoes, whether by implication or design, much of LAG's approach: 'access is achieved where individuals are aware of their need for legal services and can select and actually obtain legal services of an appropriate quality, at a price within reach'.[1]

This definition can be taken as raising some key issues about the delivery of services. These include: the importance of generating awareness of need, which LAG sees as requiring the education and information role discussed in the last chapter; the possibility of legal services being delivered in different forms than currently is the case; the importance of giving potential clients a right to choose between different providers or types of provider, and an emphasis on quality. It is not clear exactly what the board means by its final qualification 'at a price within reach'. However, services must certainly be both affordable by clients and acceptably priced for government.

Implementation of LAG's legal services approach would require a fundamental review of publicly funded legal services as a whole. At a time when there is a very real danger of a series of unrelated and largely unconsidered cuts to services resulting from the Lord Chancellor's Department's struggle to meet the demands of the Treasury, there are two pre-conditions for such a review. First, it should be established only in the context of a commitment to a broader approach to legal services. Second, it must be undertaken in the context of a search for improvement, not as a cost-cutting exercise.

Planned provision

LAG believes that services should be provided by the most effective and coherent means; but this must, of course, take existing provision into account. We envisage a mixed model of services, whereby private practitioners and other types of providers combine to ensure an overall pattern of comprehensive cover. This raises the controversial issue of salaried services.

The large-scale replacement of private practitioners by a salaried national legal service has been recently proposed by the Law Centres Federation. It argues that there should be 'a salaried service comprising independent generalist front-line advice and legal casework agencies, strategic services and specialist centres. All elements would be co-ordinated regionally and nationally.'[2] The implications of the LCF proposal are unclear. Its salaried service could be seen as ultimately taking over the role of private practitioners, even in such traditional areas of legally aided practice as matrimonial law and crime; alternatively, it could remain as an additional and supplementary provision.

LAG considers that much more use could be made of salaried services – directly employed or indirectly resourced by the funding authority – which offer various advantages, including flexibility and cost-effectiveness. However, we recognise certain pragmatic limitations to major change. First, current providers have their areas of expertise. Law centres and advice agencies have concentrated on social welfare law, while private practitioners have a wealth of experience in traditional legally aided work, particularly in the fields of crime, matrimonial and personal injury. Second, the fact that salaried services, by their very nature, offer an easy target for a government that wishes to restrict costs cannot be ignored. Their widespread introduction allows for the possibility of capping the legal services budget, moving away from the advantages, despite the present unsatisfactory eligibility levels, of the current demand-led system of legal aid expenditure. Advice agencies and law centres already face funding problems. Another example of the difficulties of salaried services is provided by the Crown Prosecution Service, which has been underfunded from its beginning and unable to recruit staff of a sufficiently high quality. Third, the wide involvement of the legal professions in the legal aid scheme has, in the past, operated to encourage the growth of legal aid – and now helps to protect it. The high financial stake many practitioners have in the scheme provides a source of articulate support for legal aid as a state-funded service, in a way that has been lacking in the field of, say, social security benefits – or in legal services in some of the foreign jurisdictions studied in Part III.

LAG's proposals are, therefore, expressly tempered by a concern to be realistic. While wishing to maximise services, we do not intend to put forward plans which provide government with the opportunity for cuts in provision. This makes us cautious about supporting any major extension of salaried services. However some restructuring is necessary, with greater priority given to the funding of advice agencies and the 'community legal centres', as discussed later in this chapter.

There is also a role for cautious experiment with salaried lawyers employed directly by a legal services authority. The Legal Aid Act 1988 does not give the Legal Aid Board a clear power to deliver advice, assistance and representative by way of its own employees. This should be amended. Some experience of direct delivery of a limited level of services would improve the board's knowledge of the practical aspects of legal aid work. A comparison of how legally aided private practice and a salaried service operate would be helpful, both in relation to quality and cost. Such an experiment should not, however, undermine the right of clients to choose to consult a private practitioner – as they can in Quebec's legal aid scheme – at least in relation to any assistance going beyond advice and immediate representation in interim matters

A possible area of work for a trial run in the use of salaried lawyers is the police station 24-hour solicitor scheme, particularly in those places where local practitioners have indicated their unwillingness to serve. The Law Society argued successfully that resources should be made available for the scheme, on the assumption that the work would be undertaken by its members in private practice. Not surprisingly, many criminal practitioners, particularly those in small firms, are now exhausted. The unsocial hours are difficult to fit into a conventional solicitors' practice, with the result that, increasingly, unqualified clerks are being sent to police stations. Recent research into criminal legal aid has raised serious questions about the service delivered to clients.[3] Salaried lawyers directly employed by the board might represent a better alternative than the currently favoured option of contracting out such provision.

There is a potential conflict for salaried lawyers between the demands of their employer, especially where this is the funder of publicly funded legal services, and their professional duty to their clients. Such a conflict exists in any situation where the lawyer acting for a client is being funded by a third party. There must be a strong professional code which binds the duties of employed lawyers as a counterbalance to the dangers of inadequate funding. This has been one of the justifications for maintaining the independence of law centres from their source of funding. The same conflict arises even with the funding of private practitioners as soon as the funding authority seeks to impose controls over what kinds of work are undertaken or resourced. This is discussed further below.

Advice services

The advice sector, which provides the first tier of service, includes an immense diversity of provision. There are over 700 CABx: these vary in size considerably, but all conform to certain national standards as a condition of membership of their national association (NACAB). The 650 members of the Federation of Independent Advice Centres represent an even more diverse group of organisations.

Thus, the sector includes such differing bodies as the small rural CAB, with its part-time manager and a largely volunteer workforce; linked complexes of CABx, highly dependent on permanent staff and managed, to some extent, as a single group (such as in Stoke-on-Trent); advice agencies, generally already with paid staff, which are seeking to fund lawyer posts through use of green form advice (like Ford and Pennywell Advice Centre in Sunderland) and even those agencies which have assimilated lawyers into their staffing complement (such as Waltham Forest or Kensington CABx). In addition, some CABx have a law centre directly attached to them (as in Paddington and Hackney). These agencies clearly vary in the level of assistance they can offer, but they are linked by a shared understanding of a common function: to encourage and deal with initial enquiries for advice and information by members of the public.

Besides this key service, many have assumed additional roles. As demonstrated in this book, particularly in the studies of employment law and debt in chapters 5 and 6, lack of provision by lawyers has encouraged advice agencies to fill what would otherwise be a gap in provision, and they have built up a specialist knowledge of such areas as social security and employment law. A number have developed ways of providing representation for their clients, at least in these two fields of social welfare law. A few agencies, such as the money advice centres that concentrate on debt and benefits, have developed highly specialist roles, thus moving away altogether from a general service.

A major strength of the advice sector has been its ability to mobilise volunteers to provide general information, diagnostic advice and referral – thousands of volunteers supplement a small nucleus of paid workers. Recent employment trends are affecting the number and type of people available for volunteering: help from the retired may be increasing, but married women are, more and more, turning to paid rather than unpaid work.[4] This may lead to a reduction in the number of volunteers, upon whom, as shown in chapter 2, the CAB service so depends. A more immediate threat to current levels of service is the chaos in local government finance, as a result of central government cuts in allowable spending and the aftermath of an ill-considered poll tax. For example, North Tyneside CABx were closed recently after their local authority was poll-tax capped.[5]

A national policy on advice agencies is long overdue. Chapter 12 argued for changes in central government funding of the national organisations representing the advice sector. Although the initiative reflected in the diversity of existing advice agencies has been a positive by-product of local funding, another, less welcome, consequence has been patchy provision. There needs to be some way of combining national standards of provision with locally determined forms.

Accordingly, there should be a statutory responsibility on local authorities to provide an adequate level of independent advice for those living and working within their areas; how such advice is best provided should be determined locally. The legal services commission, taking over an expanded role from the Legal Aid Board, should advise on a minimum acceptable level of provision, based on objective indices of need (such as local housing conditions and numbers of people on benefit), to prevent national standards being set so low that some authorities act opportunistically to cut their own existing provision. Subsidy from central government should be forthcoming for this minimum level.

More secure funding and greater national involvement in local provision raises the question of identifying and maintaining performance criteria. Adherence to such criteria, which should be linked to the needs of a particular area, not just based on a crude count of enquiries, would be a condition of funding.

Community legal centres

The term 'community legal centre' is used in this book to indicate an organisation characterised by its orientation towards serving the legal needs of its local community, particularly in those areas not served by private practice, and which also has the ability to represent its clients in every appropriate court or tribunal. The most obvious example of such a body in this country is a law centre. However, the definition might include some agencies with a practising lawyer on their staff that choose to describe themselves as advice agencies. If LAG's proposals for the development of community legal centres were implemented, existing law centres could choose whether or not to apply for funding. It would, in fact, be desirable for some law centres to remain independent of such funding in order to maintain different models of provision.

Community legal centres represent the development of one out of many strands of thought that have characterised the law centre movement since its inception. The first law centre, North Kensington, stated its aims in 1970 as providing 'a first-class solicitor's service to the people of the North Kensington community; a service which is easily accessible, not intimidating, to which they can turn for guidance as they would to their family doctor, or as someone who can afford it would turn to his family solicitor'.[6] The first major document from law centres collectively took a very different line: 'The involvement of lawyers and the provision of legal services in areas of concern to the poor and working class involves not merely a quantitative change in those legal services but also a qualitative one. As has been said: ". . . Effective solution of the [legal] problems [of the poor] may require the lawyer to direct his attention away from the particular claim or grievance to the broader interests and policies at stake, away from the individual client to a class of clients, in order to challenge more directly and with greater impact certain structural sources of injustice."'[7]

Significant developments in thought and practice have occurred since this document was published in 1974, both in this country and abroad. Ontario, Quebec, the Netherlands and Australia have all, in different ways, absorbed the law centre model into the mainstream of their provision and made available the resources for planned expansion. By contrast, shortage of resources has forced British law centres to supplement their income from legal aid, thus sometimes duplicating the work of private practitioners.

There are at least five aspects of provision which should be covered by community legal centres.

The first is to continue the law centre tradition of legal innovation. Law centres have played a pioneering role in identifying previously unrecognised areas of need. They initiated 24-hour emergency services: those relating to police stations have now been taken over by the duty solicitor scheme, but those covering civil emergencies have yet to be fully incorporated nationally. In addition, law centres have, in large part, been responsible for developing legal services in relation to the rights of tenants, immigrants and asylum-seekers, those involved in the juvenile courts and, most recently, education. Specialist centres have furthered the process of opening up new areas – in this country, these include mental health, through MIND's legal department, and social security law, through the Child Poverty Action Group. Abroad, there are the examples of Australia's Public Interest Advocacy Centre and Ontario's Advisory Resource Center for the Handicapped. A clear statement of this role comes from Redfern Legal Centre in Sydney: 'To investigate and develop new ways of providing legal services . . . in the interests of improving access to . . . services and to ensure that the quality of those services is maintained and improved.'[8]

The second aspect of a community legal centre is its orientation to the particular needs of its local community. Law centres have sought to do this in various ways. Great emphasis has been placed on community management – and on accessibility, as reflected in the aim of North Kensington quoted above. This approach informs a recent definition of a law centre in a 1991 Law Society working paper: 'Law centres are publicly funded, non-profit making organisations which provide legal advice and assistance to poor and disadvantaged neighbourhoods which might otherwise not have access to the law or have the means to pay for legal services.'

A third role is to focus on under-resourced areas of social welfare law. Belfast Law Centre recently announced the result of internal discussions on its function: 'We have now clarified our role as being to promote the enforcement and development of social welfare law. We have defined our areas of work as being social security, housing, debt/money advice, employment, immigration and (in the future) mental health.'[9] This is a classic list of law centre concerns. The Law Centres Federation has its own list of 'the most common areas of work' undertaken by law centres, which includes: 'housing (eg tenants rights); welfare rights/debt; employment (eg industrial tribunals); planning and environment; children's rights; nationality and immigration; disabled people's rights; homelessness; mental health; juvenile crime; care, wardship, child abuse; women's rights; discrimination (eg race, sex and sexuality); education'.[10]

A fourth aspect is to build upon the approach found in many law centres which, at its best, combines the elements that LAG sees as crucial to the comprehensive provision of legal services: advice, assistance and representation; legal education, and law reform. Areas of social welfare law, which tend to have both a high administrative and a public policy component, as well as being directed towards the most deprived sectors of society, are particularly well suited to this multi-faceted approach.

Finally, community legal centres, based on current practice within law centres, would have tremendous advantages in dealing with the need for tribunal representation. The Legal Aid Board has already noted this: 'law centres employ both specialist staff who can conduct tribunal representation which is outside the scope of legal aid, and lawyers able to identify judicial review points which is within scope. This provides an ideal combination of staffing, rarely found elsewhere, to bridge the gap for this kind of work.'[11] In LAG's view, community legal centres represent a much more cost-effective way of providing representation for tribunals than would result from an extension of legal aid, for precisely the reasons noted by the board – namely, their legal expertise and mix of legal and lay staff.

Despite recognising the value of law centres, the Legal Aid Board has given three reasons why it should not be responsible for their funding:

- law centres concentrate on work which is outside the scope of legal aid. It would be self-contradictory for the board to pay law centres for doing work it is not prepared to pay other agencies or solicitors' practices to do;
- law centres' activities in relation to local issues and problems should be funded from and evaluated by local sources;
- the best guarantee of law centres being able to continue their innovative work lies in the security that would be provided by mixed funding.[12]

These reasons are not persuasive. First, government should broaden its perception of legal aid – even if the Legal Aid Board cannot – so as to include tribunal representation. This, as we argue in chapter 12, is a pressing need. Second, the work of law centres is only 'local' in that each centre's geographical area of activity is necessarily determined by its location – as is that of any legal aid solicitor's practice. Their essential function of meeting local gaps in nationally funded provision is one which should be nationally recognised. Evaluation of their effectiveness may require local investigation, but that does not imply that funding must be local. Third, mixed funding may be ideal, but it is irrelevant if no partner will come forward and undesirable if it is accepted that centres carry out their activities as part of a national policy on legal services.

The government and board should reverse their funding policy. The board needs to develop a system of published criteria under which grant aid would be available to legal centres and by which their performance would be evaluated. Appendix 2 illustrates how other jurisdictions have approached this question, providing the basis from which to develop such criteria. From these examples, it is clear that community legal centres would need an effective management structure in order to qualify. Like existing law centres, they must remain autonomous, with their own management committees. Greater accountability would come through the need to comply with performance criteria.

One barrier to the extension of law centres during the 1980s was the concern by government that they take too 'political' an approach. This accusation has dogged law centres from their early days. The Royal Commission on Legal Services was much exercised by their supposedly political and campaigning role, and its own proposed 'citizens' law centres' were designed to be resolutely non-political and non-campaigning.[13] This should not remain a serious concern. Political parameters are, in fact, easily established, along with the development of performance evaluation, linked to funding, to counteract accusations of non-accountability.

Another concern of the Royal Commission was the lack of adequate employment terms for those working in law centres. It recommended that 'there should be a national career structure, national salary rates and a national pension scheme'.[14] Research in 1983 found that 'the low morale of most workers in law centres (there are a few exceptions) is a major problem' and that this led to a high turnover of staff.[15] Part of the problem stemmed from financial problems, and these have become considerably worse since then. The funding of most law centres is insecure; consequently, so are law centre jobs.

The problem of pay and conditions must be addressed. The Legal Aid Board should establish national guidelines for remuneration that are equivalent to those of government salaried employees, as has recently occurred in Ontario. The development of more management or co-ordinator posts, not necessarily restricted to lawyers, and of more specialist law centres, could offer the basis of a rudimentary career structure.

A planned national network of community legal centres should be phased in gradually. This would avoid too great an initial expenditure, while also ensuring that centres are established only where adequate preparatory work has been done. Some new funding is inevitable, though a degree of offset might come from a transfer from existing green form costs. One of the functions of the comprehensive review of provision proposed earlier would be to suggest ways of finding the necessary resources.

Each community legal centre should employ at least three lawyers, two non-lawyer practitioners and two support staff. Volunteer legal advisers have played a vital role in assisting law centres, particularly in evening advice sessions. This tradition, which has not only provided a source of free labour but has also involved private practitioners in the voluntary sector, should continue, as should training and use of volunteer lay advisers. The exact range of services provided by each community legal centre, (which will depend, in part, on what is already available in the area) will have to be negotiated through the kind of local planning process that Belfast Law Centre has already experimented with in Northern Ireland. The overall objective is, however, quite clear: advice agencies and the community legal centre in an area should, between them, provide a comprehensive range of services within social welfare law.

The community legal centres should receive core funding to provide specified minimum levels of service, not only in relation to advice, assistance and representation, but also in the field of legal education and appropriate law reform activity. The presence of a central funding authority in the planning of this process would introduce a new dimension to the existing position, in which the majority of law centres are accountable only at a local level.

Core funding should be sufficient for the community legal centres to follow the voluntary advice sector tradition of acting without charge for all clients, thus providing the free element in essential legal services. Furthermore, the centres should be the vehicle by which representation is extended before tribunals. With a mix of lay and legally qualified practitioners, they will have the ability to provide the appropriate levels of representation in any case. Such a system would clearly be more economic than a wholesale extension of legal aid. However, at least one firm of private practitioners should also be encouraged, by franchise or other means, to provide a service in this area. As well as giving clients an element of choice, this would provide some measure of competition and comparison; it would also provide a safeguard against community legal centre staff becoming overworked, to the detriment of clients.

Community legal centre lawyers should be able to claim legal aid on a case-by-case basis for cases falling within their general areas of competence but outside the tribunal system, though they should be under a general injunction not to take such cases simply to raise finance.

Eventually, a network of community legal centres should cover the whole country. As a first step, a sufficient number should be established both to test and refine the idea. A reasonable target might be for the Legal Aid Board to fund 90 community legal centres, phased in over three years. A centre of the minimum size envisaged above would cost about £330,000 per year on current rates. So, in crude terms, establishing 30 in each of the next three years would require expenditure of £10 million in the first year, £20 million in the second and £30 million in the third. To start with, centres should be situated in poorer areas not currently covered by private practitioners doing social welfare law work. In some cases, rather than start a centre from scratch, an existing law centre may wish to transfer to the new regime. The law centre movement should not, however, be expected to transfer wholesale.

Community legal centres should be encouraged to maintain an innovative approach to services and their core funding should include basic provision for both the education and law reform functions discussed in chapter 12. This should be supplemented by a special project fund (of, say, an initial £5 million), for which community legal centres and other agencies could bid each year to resource innovative projects similar to those supported by the New South Wales Law Foundation (see p100).

Specialist law centres

Funding should also be made available for specialist law centres to provide back-up services such as information for advisers, nationally co-ordinated educational campaigns, law reform activity, specialist advice, and a resource for helping with, or taking over, the more complex and time-consuming cases. Such centres stimulate the quality of the work of all practitioners in their fields, as has been shown in Ontario and Australia, where they have been funded through the legal aid schemes. In the area of housing, for example, a centre of excellence in housing law should be funded, perhaps building on an existing organisation, such as the National Housing Law Service, which has struggled to provide a similar sort of service without adequate core funding, or Shelter, the best-known campaigning organisation in the field. Consumer credit law (p62) has been discussed elsewhere in this book as an example of an area that would benefit from a specialist service.

Private practice

Private practitioners should continue as the main providers of services in the field of matrimonial and family work, crime and personal injury, as well as having some involvement in other areas of law. Three particular issues need to be addressed in relation to the use of private practitioners: planning, quality and remuneration.

Planning

The use of private practitioners to deliver legal aid services has resulted in uneven provision, both geographically and in the areas of law covered. Even if the legal aid system is retained in its present form, the pattern of solicitors' practices is likely to change radically in the near future, resulting in a greater concentration of resources and more specialisation. A number of factors could contribute to this. First, the solicitors' conveyancing monopoly – traditionally, the mainstay of many general practices – is still under threat. Its loss could accelerate the existing trend towards more specialised practices. Some of these may concentrate on legal aid work, but others could move away from it, leaving some areas without access to general legal aid services.

Second, the reform of rights of audience in the higher courts is likely to alter the nature of legal aid practice, particularly in criminal work. Solicitors will be attracted by the opportunity to develop their advocacy skills in jury trials and the increased possibility of ultimate judicial appointment, which would counteract the low status, and mitigate the relatively low pay, of such work.

This could affect sizeable criminal practices in one of two ways. On the one hand, it could counteract the trend over recent years whereby these firms have to take, for economic reasons, ever-increasing volumes of routine representation in magistrates' courts, which means delegating important out-of-court services (police station advice, preparatory and investigatory work on cases) to unqualified and, in many instances, poorly trained staff. Instead, a more balanced practice could develop, in which volume was exchanged for in-depth work on fewer cases with a view to seeing them through, to a high professional standard, from the beginning at detention in a police station to final hearing at a Crown Court trial.

On the other hand, there is a real danger that bureaucratic tendencies in the organisation of private criminal defence firms would be further entrenched, with senior practitioners simply 'upgrading' their status by taking on more advocacy in the Crown Court (short trials, guilty pleas), possibly even taking on this work from other firms, and delegating even more vital preparatory and investigatory work to less qualified and lower paid staff.

Which line the profession follows will, to some extent, depend on developments in the administration of legal aid and the form of remuneration – illustrating yet again the need for strategic planning when law and procedure reforms are being considered, and the necessity of sufficiently strong quality controls.

The combined effect of these changes means that reliance on market forces may prove an even more unreliable way of delivering services than at present. The Legal Aid Board is seeking to introduce an element of planning into the provision of legal aid through its experiment with franchising green form advice. Ultimately, it sees this as a way of concentrating resources on larger providers. In its first consultation paper on franchising, it explicitly stated that this was its goal: 'if the Board was satisfied that franchising provided sufficient access for consumers in a given locality, the existing green form scheme could be discontinued in that locality.'[16]

The board is correct to move towards a system where provision can be better planned. Services in some areas of the country may be improved if legal aid were channelled through a smaller number of higher quality providers: one example is criminal work in certain inner city areas. However, some mechanism must remain whereby new practices can break into the market.

In looking for greater control over where and how legal services are provided, the board's starting point should be to ask whether the existing pattern of services provides acceptable access to legal services. In support of its own definition of what is acceptable (see p133), it should draw up criteria setting minimum levels of provision. There is some indication that, in its work on access, it is now doing so.[17]

If sufficient legal aid outlets do not exist, it must create them. It could do this through a range of measures, including grant aid towards the establishment costs of private practices, enhanced rates of legal aid remuneration or the setting up of a branch office with salaried lawyers or some form of mobile community legal centre.

Restrictions on access must also be considered in other terms. Barriers such as class and race have to be overcome. To counterbalance a largely white, middle-class legal profession, it may be necessary to deploy advice agencies or community legal centres whose workers and work practices are more accessible to specific groups in the community.

Quality

LAG believes that all solicitors and barristers should, in principle, be entitled to act for a legally aided client. This is an important guarantee, not least of the operation of a market sufficiently open to allow the entry of new practitioners. However, conditions should be imposed on the quality of the work of any lawyer who wishes to undertake a legally aided case. These should include a requirement to demonstrate sufficient regularity of practice to maintain knowledge and skills in the relevant area. This need not, necessarily, be gained in legally aided practice.

To meet LAG's objective of equal access to justice, the quality of publicly funded legal services should match that available to private clients. Without this, there can be no equality for a publicly funded litigant. In cases where the legally aided client faces an opponent with legal services of the highest quality – for example, in serious criminal cases or civil cases against the government, where the state deploys an effectively unlimited budget – equivalent services must be available to both sides.

In its pilot franchising project, the board has put considerable energy into the idea of using franchising as a tool to monitor and, thereby, improve quality. LAG shares the board's concern about the quality of legal aid practice: much of this is excellent, but some is below an acceptable standard. In particular, the standard of criminal defence work needs scrutiny. As the funding agency, however, the board has a potential conflict of interest. It may be concerned to raise quality; it is definitely interested in restraining costs. At a certain point, the two must become incompatible.

While the board should be encouraged to explore what quality criteria it can impose on practitioners directly through its franchising contract, this potential conflict of interest would be ameliorated if the Law Society played a greater role. The Society should agree quality criteria with the board and promulgate these in codes of practice. A requirement of adherence to these codes should then be included in the board's contracts with its providers; breach of them would be a professional, disciplinary matter leading to the loss of accredited status to undertake legally aided work.

The Law Society has proved reluctant to take all but minimal powers in relation to the quality regulation of its members. This is a mistake; the Society needs to maintain its position as the guarantor of the independence of its members. A greater commitment to quality would also assist its bargaining position with government on remuneration, for it would give force to its argument that some types of case can only be handled satisfactorily if certain standards, involving time and expertise, are met. The danger in ceding the drawing up of quality criteria to a funding body is that the latter, driven by its concern to restrain expenditure, will increasingly limit the exercise of professional judgment a practitioner can deploy on behalf of a client. For instance, time allowed for the search for an elusive witness, and the approach to be undertaken in a particular type of case, may come to be prescribed, thereby potentially damaging the quality of the defence case.

Moreover, enforcement of quality criteria should not be left solely to the funding authority; again, considerations of cost could affect its judgment. A separate inspectorate to guarantee and adjudicate quality standards should be established. Such an inspectorate could be developed out of an amalgamation of the Solicitors' Complaints Board and the office of the Legal Services Ombudsman. This would require the Law Society to relinquish control over its complaints procedure, and for this to become fully independent – a move which LAG has long argued is, in any event, necessary.

Remuneration

Legal aid remuneration to private practitioners is currently being hotly debated. It must be tackled properly to ensure an adequate level of service to clients. For the Legal Aid Board to be involved in quality control, but play no role in the remuneration debate, is unsatisfactory. The Legal Aid Act 1988 requirement that the Lord Chancellor consult with the representative bodies of the profession over remuneration levels must be extended to include the board.

Current debate is focused on the method of payment, with the Law Society arguing that it must be based on time expended, rather than through the fixed fee system which the Lord Chancellor is seeking to extend to new areas. The underlying question, however, concerns the level of remuneration. There is no easy answer to this. Legal aid practitioners will always tend to demand more than any government is willing to give. But there must be a yardstick by which acceptable levels of remuneration are judged. At the moment, neither side will state openly what it thinks is reasonable. The Law Society should declare its expectations of what a legal aid practitioner, working an efficient and set number of hours per week, should receive as net 'take-home' pay. The government should set comparable levels for full-time legal aid practitioners. This can be approached in a number of ways: by reference to other publicly funded professionals, such as doctors and dentists; by reference to the rate for a lawyer acting for private clients, or by reference to what the government pays the lawyers in its employ. There is a danger that any divergence from private rates may create a second-class service because the best lawyers will go for the highest paid jobs. Nevertheless, remuneration by reference to the pay of government salaried lawyers seems more realistic. But to this should be added an element for the extra responsibility of running a business, thus maintaining an indirect link with market rates.

Once such figures are produced, progress can then be made on the formula whereby the gross income of a solicitors's practice might lead to the intended net goal. The basis of funding might be similar to the allowances available to general practitioner doctors.

Negotiations on such a delicate subject as remuneration will never be easy and no system of payment is perfect. Time-costing subsidises inefficiency and gives no incentive for expertise and speed, while fixed fees without quality controls reward the quick rather than the thorough. Without adequate safeguards of quality, the latter should not be extended. Ultimately, however the profession is remunerated, if there is to be equal access to justice, there must be enforceable codes of practice that inhibit bad practice in the preparation of the cases of legally aided clients.

Conclusion

The ultimate goal must be to provide publicly funded services in the most effective way. This can only be done in the context of the reforms set out in both of the previous two chapters. LAG's proposals are presented as four parts of a coherent whole. These are:

- a redefinition of the objectives of policy and firm statements of principle;
- organisational and administrative changes to implement a more integrated approach to the provision of services;
- informed decision and planning about which ways of delivering services are best suited to clients;
- an approach that integrates the consideration and reform of legal services provision with that of procedure and substantive law.

Fundamentally, the focus must move away from system geared to the legal profession as provider – the dominating influence of which has been evident in the development of publicly funded legal services so far –

towards the client both as consumer and, more broadly, as a member of society holding basic and enforceable rights.

References

1 Legal Aid Board *Annual Report 1990–91* HC 513, HMSO, para 8.1.
2 Law Centres Federation *Review of Financial Conditions for Civil Legal Aid: the Law Centre view* LCF, 1991.
3 *Independent on Sunday* 12 July 1992.
4 See April 1987 *Legal Action* 6.
5 National Association of Citizens Advice Bureaux *Annual Report 1990/91* p5.
6 C Robinson, T Chakraborty, C Dabezies *Coming of Age: North Kensington law centre 1970–1988* North Kensington Law Centre, 1988, p11.
7 *Towards Equal Justice* Law Centres Working Group, 1974, para 2.8.
8 Redfern Legal Centre *Annual Report 1989–90*.
9 Belfast Law Centre *Annual Review 1990–91*.
10 *Law Centres: a national resource worth fighting for* Law Centres Federation, 1990.
11 As in 1, para 8.14.
12 As in 1 above, para 8.15.
13 The Royal Commission on Legal Services *Final Report, volume 1* Cmnd 7648, HMSO, 1979, paras 8.17–37.
14 As in 13, para 8.31(a).
15 Law Centres Federation Evaluation Sub-committee *Law Centre Staff Research Project* 1983.
16 Legal Aid Board *Second Stage Consultation on the Future of the Green Form Scheme* May 1989, para 34.
17 Legal Aid Board *Annual Report 1991–92* HC 50, HMSO, 1992, chapter 6.

CHAPTER 15

Recommendations

1 The overall objective of publicly funded legal services is to achieve equal access to justice for all members of society and to ensure that any dispute is settled on the basis of the intrinsic merit of the arguments of the different parties, uninfluenced by any inequalities of wealth or power (pp111–13).

2 Equal access to justice should be pursued by 'a legal services approach' which combines:

a) advice, assistance and representation
b) education and information
c) reform of law and procedure. (p112)

3 Advice, assistance and representation require comprehensive services provided by:

a) legal aid private practitioners
b) law and legal centres
c) advice agencies
d) enforcement agencies, such as the Health and Safety Executive and the Commission for Racial Equality.
e) directly salaried services. (pp115, 116–18)

4 Education and information on legal rights and duties should be identified as a priority in the context of an increasing concern with the concept of citizenship and the content of the Citizen's Charter. In consequence, the Legal Aid Board, or a legal services commission, should assume a public legal education function. (pp113–15)

5 Reform of law, procedure and publicly funded legal services must be seen as integrally linked. The board should take a more active role in both initiating projects and debating proposals for law reform. All new legislation should be accompanied by a statement of its potential impact on publicly funded legal services. (pp115–16)

6 Publicly funded legal services providing advice, assistance and representation should incorporate the following:

    a) a first tier of free and non-means tested diagnostic advice and referral

    b) the free and non-means tested provision of certain essential legal services

    c) a greater priority than currently to social welfare law

    d) adequate representation at tribunals. (pp116–21)

7 Tests for financial eligibility, where appropriate, should be integrated so that a common method of calculation is applied throughout the progress of a case from advice to representation. This should be based on the current green form eligibility test and, except in complicated cases, be conducted by the solicitor.

8 Eligibility in civil cases should be extended as far as possible. Contributions should be lowered from one-quarter to one-fifth of available assets. Eligibility levels for particular types of cases, such as those relating to personal injury, should be raised immediately where this does not involve much extra cost. There should be a discretionary upper limit. (pp119–20)

9 Criminal legal aid should be free and non-means tested for any unconvicted defendant facing the possibility of imprisonment. The possibility of any meaningful reduction of current criminal legal aid expenditure is dependent on the reduction in the numbers of such defendants. (pp120–21)

10 Publicly funded legal representation through legal aid, or otherwise, should immediately be made available for hearings:

    a) before coroners

    b) before social security commissioners

    c) at the immigration appeal tribunal. (p121)

11 A minister in the House of Commons should take over responsibility for the administration of the courts and legal aid from the Lord Chancellor's Department and for the funding of voluntary sector advice agencies from the Department of Trade and Industry. A judicial commission should take over the role of appointing judges. (pp124–27)

12 A legal services commission should replace the Legal Aid Board. Its functions should be:

    a) to ensure the provision of advice, assistance and representation of such a quality that every member of society has equal access to justice

b) to initiate and carry out educational programmes designed to promote an understanding by the public, or by sections of the public, of their rights, powers, privileges and duties under the law

c) to monitor the effect of the law and the legal system, particularly in those areas most relevant to those who are the clients of publicly funded legal services, and to initiate or respond to proposals for law reform

d) to undertake research into all aspects of legal aid including investigation and assessment of different methods of financing providing publicly funded legal service.   (pp127–28)

13 The Commission should have a membership of 12 composed of:

a) five members chosen on the basis of their 'expertise in or knowledge of the provision of legal services, education, the work of the courts and social conditions or management'. No more than three would, however, be appointed on the basis of management experience or knowledge alone. At least two should have some knowledge of education.

b) seven members based on nominations made from a range of bodies representing consumers and providers of publicly funded legal services.   (pp128–29)

14 The Lord Chancellor's Advisory Committee on Legal Aid should be abolished and, failing the appointment of a legal services commission, its policy discussion role subsumed into the Legal Aid Board.
                                                                      (pp129–30)

15 Regional legal services committees should be extended to cover the country.   (p131)

16 Services should be reviewed so that they are provided through a mixed model which includes the best combination of legal aid practitioners, salaried lawyers, law and legal centres and advice agencies. There should be experimentation with salaried services.   (pp133, 135)

17 There must be a clear national policy on advice provision. Local authorities should be under a statutory duty to provide an adequate service; the cost should be recognised as essential by central government.   (p137)

18 A network of community legal centres should be established. These should specialise in the fields of social welfare law and, in particular, provide tribunal representation. They should also be funded at a level

which allows them to experiment with innovative services appropriate to their local community and to be involved in the three elements of publicly funded legal services set out in recommendation 2. (pp141–43)

19 There should be a pilot programme involving £10 million in the first year, £20 million in the second and £30 million in the third to establish 30 new community legal centres a year. There should be an additional fund of £5 million for special projects. (p143)

20 A number of specialist law centres should also be established.

21 The Legal Aid Board, or legal services commission, must take action to ensure adequate access to legal services over the whole of England and Wales. Where services are lacking, their provision should be encouraged by a range of measures such as establishment grants to private practitioners, enhanced rates of payment or assistance with branch office expenses. (p145)

22 In principle, any solicitor or barrister should be free to act for a legally aided client. The Legal Aid Board, or legal services commission, may, however, specify that services should be of a sufficiently high quality. The Law Society and other professional bodies should take steps, for example by specialist panel schemes established on criteria agreed by the legal aid funding body, to ensure that this is the case. (pp146–47)

23 The remuneration debate between the legal profession and the Lord Chancellor should concentrate on open discussion of what final income an efficient practitioner should receive. This might be linked, perhaps by a percentage uplift for the responsibilities of private practice, to the remuneration of lawyers employed by government. A formula by which this remuneration might be attained should then be decided upon. (pp147–48)

24 The focus of publicly funded legal services must change from the legal profession as the provider of legal aid to the client as the consumer of publicly funded legal services and, more broadly, as a member of society holding basic and enforceable rights. This involves:

- redefinition of the objectives of policy
- organisational and administrative changes to implement a more integrated approach
- better planning of services so that they are delivered in the way which is best suited to their recipients
- the integrated consideration of the reform of legal services, procedure and substantive law. (p148)

Appendices

Civil legal aid eligibility estimates 1979–90

Extract from a paper by Michael Murphy, London School of Economics

The tables in this appendix give updated estimates for the proportions and numbers of households and people eligible for legal advice and assistance and civil legal aid on income grounds for the period from mid 1979 up to mid 1989, based on an analysis of the 1979 and 1989 Family Expenditure Surveys (FES) and estimates for 1990 based on inflation indices.

The methodology is the same as used previously and described in detail in the document *Legal aid eligibility – calculation and interpretation of recent trends* (1989) and the article based upon it published in *Legal Action*, October 1989, pp7–8. These provided estimates based on the FES for the period 1979–87 and estimates based on inflation for the period 1987/89.

It has become impossible to make single estimates of eligibility because of two changes to the limits which came into force in April 1990. There is now a separate and higher upper limit of income eligibility for civil legal aid in personal injury cases. The resources of children are no longer aggregated with those of their parents when assessing the child's entitlement to legal aid.

The tables below give summary figures and grossed-up estimates of the number of households and persons eligibile (that is, those 'simple' households which form a single legal aid assessment unit). It has been assumed that the remaining 15 per cent or so of 'complex' households have the same eligibility as those for which estimates may be made.

Legal advice and assistance

Between 1979 and 1990, the estimated proportion of households entitled on income grounds dropped by 25.3 per cent, from 69.7 per cent to 44.2 per cent. This fall represented 15.3 million people, so that only 37 per cent of the population was covered, compared to 66.2 per cent in mid 1979. Between 1987 and 1990, the numbers eligible fell by 5.3 million people.

There are no accurate figures on which estimates of eligibility on the basis of capital holdings can be made for the relevant period. Because the capital limit is very low for advice and assistance, it is likely that the number actually ineligible is much higher than the figures given above, although no assessment can be given for the magnitude of change in this period.

It should be noted that there are no separate income limits for advice and assistance in personal injury matters; nor are children normally assessed separately from their parents.

Civil legal aid

Between 1979 and 1989, the estimated proportion of households eligible for civil legal aid declined from 80.9 per cent to 54.1 per cent, a fall of 4.3 million. During the same period, the proportion of the population eligible fell from 79.1 per cent to 48.4 per cent, a drop of over 30 per cent, representing some 16 million people.

Eligibility appears to have fallen even more substantially for the period 1987/89 than the estimates made in the article mentioned above. This was because there was an increase of 8 per cent in the legal aid limits between 1987 and 1989, but a 20 per cent increase in earnings, combined with a reduction of 2 per cent in the basic rate of income tax, in 1988. As disposable income rose over these years, so the proportions eligible fell substantially for the working-age groups.

As with legal advice and assistance, the effect of the capital limits will be to reduce eligibility even further than the figures quoted above.

The position since 1989

Two important changes in income eligibility occurred in 1990 (a complicating factor for 1990 is the replacement of the married woman's tax allowance). Children became eligible in their own right and differential and higher eligibility levels were introduced in personal injury cases. These changes need to be assessed by comparison with the position relating to households generally, where an adult living in a family may apply for aid. In these cases, ineligibility may well affect the financial position of the whole family, since the failure of one or both parents to secure legal aid because of ineligibility on income grounds – for example, for a disabling personal injury – may have a direct effect on the whole family. For these reasons, the overall figures for eligibility may continue to be relevant. It can be estimated that during the period 1979/90 some 4.7 million households, representing 17.6 million people, went out of scope for these purposes.

Children

The effect of the 1990 change is to make virtually all children eligible for legal aid in their own right. In 1979, 79.8 per cent of all children (about 11 million) were eligible when their parents' resources were aggregated with their own. By 1989 this figure had fallen to 45.8 per cent (about 5 million children). The net effect of the change, therefore, was to bring about 7 million more children within the scope of the scheme, principally for personal injury cases.

Adults

The limits were raised by about 5 per cent in April 1990. Over the previous year, prices and earnings rose by about 10 per cent; the tax position was broadly neutral. Thus, the eligibility level fell about 5 per cent in real terms. Sensitivity analysis of the 1989 data suggests that a reduction of 1 per cent in the real levels of the limit would lead to about 0.5 per cent fewer adults being eligible for legal aid, although the effect would be more substantial for parents. Between April 1989 and April 1990, it can be estimated that a further 1.1 million adults fell outside the scope of the scheme.

Personal injury limit

It was suggested that the enhanced limit for these cases – £7,000 rather than £6,350 – would lead to a considerable increase in the numbers of those obtaining access to the legal aid scheme. It is noteworthy, however, that if the upper limit had kept pace with earnings since 1987 – the appropriate way of uprating in order to keep the proportion of the population approximately fixed – the 1990 limit would actually have been over £7,000. The effect of this uprating is only to put the eligibility level at somewhat below that of 1987. In April 1990, the increased personal injury level meant that only 5.6 per cent more adults (or 2.4 million people) qualified than in respect of other forms of legal aid.

Table A: Estimates of proportions and numbers of persons eligible for legal advice and assistance, Great Britain 1979/90

(i) Households* (millions)

	Number	Percentage eligible	Eligible	Ineligible
1979	19.7	69.7	13.7	6.0
1982	20.3	65.3	13.2	7.0
1987	21.2	52.7	11.2	10.0
1988	21.4	47.6	10.2	11.2
1989	21.6	46.2	10.0	11.6
1990	21.8	44.2	9.6	12.2

(ii) Persons (millions)

	Number	Percentage eligible	Eligible	Ineligible
1979	54.3	66.2	36.0	18.4
1982	54.8	61.8	33.9	20.9
1987	55.4	47.0	26.0	29.3
1988	55.5	40.8	22.6	32.8
1989	55.7	39.2	21.8	33.8
1990	55.8	37.0	20.7	35.1

Sources for households data: *Social Trends* 1982 and 1989, table 2.5.

*Complex households are assumed to have average simple household value for eligibility.

Table B: Estimates of proportions and numbers of persons eligible for civil legal aid, Great Britain 1979/90

(i) Households* (millions)

	Number	Percentage eligible	Eligible	Ineligible
1979	19.7	80.9	15.9	3.8
1982	20.3	77.1	15.6	4.6
1987	21.2	61.2	13.0	8.2
1988	21.4	56.0	12.0	9.4
1989	21.6	54.1	11.7	9.9
1990	21.8	51.5	11.2	10.6
1990†	21.8	56.8	12.4	9.4

(ii) Persons (millions)

	Number	Percentage eligible	Eligible	Ineligible
1979	54.3	79.1	43.0	11.4
1982	54.8	75.6	41.4	13.4
1987	55.4	57.2	31.7	23.7
1988	55.5	50.4	28.0	27.5
1989	55.7	48.4	27.0	28.7
1990	55.8	45.4	25.4	30.4
1990†	55.8	51.2	28.6	27.2

Sources for households data: *Social Trends* 1982 and 1989, table 2.5.

*Complex households are assumed to have average simple household value for eligibility.

†Personal injury only.

Legal clinic and centres' performance evaluation criteria (Ontario, Canada and Australia)

Extract from the Clinic performance evaluation criteria Ontario Clinic Funding Committee (in force April 1991)

I   *Overall and fundamental criteria*

1   The clinic provides a range of client services, as described in the Regulation on clinic funding.

2   The clinic provides legal intervention, advocacy, and litigation at many levels of the administrative/judicial decision-making process.

3   The composition of the Board of Directors reflects a balance of low-income representatives, independent legal skills, financial skills, and experience working in community-based groups.

4   The Board of Directors is independent of other community groups and of its staff.

5   Members of the Board of Directors actively take responsibility for the management of clinic services.

6   Financial procedures, financial controls, and reporting procedures are sound.

7   The intake system, case assignment system, the assignment of other clinic work, and the overall organization of staff make efficient use of staff time and abilities.

8   The clinic has in place a system of annual planning and evaluation.

II   *Information gathering*

9   The Board of Directors has documented the need for legal services for low income people in the community served by the clinic, particularly taking into account circumstances in the local community and other services available to low income people.

10 The clinic has a method of gathering information regarding current trends and changing cultural/economic patterns in the community, for use in planning.

III Planning

11 The Board of Directors of the clinic sets priorities for client services within the overall clinic mandate, which recognize the highest needs for legal services in the low income community served by the clinic.

12 The clinic articulates clear measurable objectives for client services based on the priorities of the Board of Directors, and assigns activities to achieve each objective.

13 Initial and ongoing staff training is adequate and appropriate.

14 The general clinic takes into account the services and expertise provided by specialty clinics when planning the clinic's priorities.

15 The clinic is responding to current trends and changing cultural/economic patterns which affect the legal needs of low income people in the community served by the clinic by regularly reviewing local economic and demographic factors and appropriately updating or revising priorities for clinic services, as is necessary.

IV Action/implementation

16 Activities in all areas of client services, including casework, public legal education, law reform, and community organizing are integrated to reflect the priorities established by the Board of Directors and to achieve maximum impact of the clinic services in those areas of priority.

17 The job descriptions and staffing ratios adopted by the Board of Directors are designed to meet the staffing needs of the clinic programs.

18 The clinic utilizes its physical facilities efficiently, including satellite offices, hours of operation and access by the public, use of equipment, use of space and initiatives to control costs.

19 Supervision procedures are appropriate for the needs of the clinic and are applied to all legal services provided.

20 The tickler system [date reminder system] meets the standards required by the Law Society of Upper Canada, and is appropriate to the particular needs of the clinic.

21 Client confidentiality is respected during intake procedures, file management procedures, and telephone and personal interview procedures.

22 The general clinics use the services and expertise provided by specialty clinics.

23 Orientation and training of new Board members is carried out.

V Evaluation services/programs

24 The Board of Directors regularly reviews clinic activities in casework, law reform, community organizing, and public legal education, and reviews short and long term plans to achieve clinic objectives. The Board of Directors will have in place management systems such as information systems, a staff evaluation procedure, and Board management systems and structure.

VI   *Evaluation board effectiveness. Accountability to community*

25 The clinic's complaint procedures allow for the unobstructed expression and resolution of complaints about any aspect of the clinic.

26 The Board of Directors has developed a process for making the public and other agencies aware of clinic services; i.e. the clinic has a stable or expanding membership base or the clinic can demonstrate community support by attendance at general meetings or other evidence.

27 The Board reviews the level of community awareness and support for the clinic from time to time.

28 The clinic is able to attract and keep members of the Board of Directors.

29 The Board of Directors makes use of its Executive Committee structure to allow productive use of meeting time.

Extract from Guidelines: Commonwealth Funding Program for Community Legal Centres *Ministry of the Attorney-General, Australia (in force July 1991)*

Eligibility criteria

7.1.   A centre must be constituted in a formal manner (but not necessarily incorporated), be a non-profit organization, and, have management and control independent of State or Commonwealth government and professional bodies and be structured so as to ensure that it is responsive to the needs of the community.

7.2.   A centre must have a demonstrated financial need taking into account all recurrent funding. (A reasonable carry over for contingencies or reserves may be allowed for in assessing financial need.)

7.3.   It is highly desirable that a centre engage in innovative projects, especially those aimed at the development of cost effective legal care services and preventive legal aid.

7.4.   As general principles:* the primary purpose of a centre should be the provision of legal care services (eg, advice, referral, duty lawyer, casework and test cases), although the Commonwealth acknowledges the value of, and encourages, other activities (eg, law reform, community legal education and 'outreach' programs); and

7.5.   A centre should be able to demonstrate a community need for its objectives and services whether that community be geographic or a special client/special interest community.

7.6.   A centre must be, or seek to be, 'community based' by being accessible (in the broadest sense of the term) to the community it aims to serve and should,

---

*   Centres undertaking a high volume of casework will normally be funded at a higher level than centres undertaking lower cost legal services.

therefore, plan its location, premises, hours of business, and nature and structure of staff, around that objective.

7:7 A centre must be an outcome of initiative by the community but, for the purposes of this Guideline, the term 'community' is not confined to the definitions at Guideline 1.3 (which apply elsewhere throughout the Guidelines), but includes the community 'at large'.

7.8. As a general rule, a centre should have and maintain a high level of voluntary input. In any event a centre must demonstrate that it has taken every reasonable step to encourage the involvement of existing and prospective volunteers. However, it is recognized by the Commonwealth that some centres, because of their geographical location or other special circumstances, may not be able to achieve significant levels in the number of volunteers.

Financial accountability

8.1. Evidence must be provided to State commissions by previously funded centres to show that the purposes for which a grant was made, were, or are, being met. This would normally take the form of a short certificate signed by the executive of a centre.

8.2. Centres must supply to State commissions copies of their audited financial statements as soon as possible after the end of the previous funding period (save that a commission may in the case of centres receiving small grants – as determined by the commission in accordance with the accounting practice or audit requirements of the relevant commission – only require a financial statement certified on behalf of the management committee as being full and accurate).

They must also supply such financial statements (audited or not) as State commissions may reasonably require in the performance of their functions under this Program. Consequently a centre may be required to produce an (unaudited) financial statement in the early stages of the evaluation process of the Program. If, in the opinion of a State commission, a centre has not provided a copy of its audited or certified financial statement within a reasonable time following the end of the accounting year for the centre, then the commission will withhold payment of the next six monthly advance for that centre until such time as a satisfactory audited or certified financial statement is provided.

In effect this means that if a centre prepares financial statements on a calendar year basis then the cheque would be withheld if there were no audit report or certified financial statement by 31 December.

8.3. Audit certificates must be given by a qualified public accountant who is not an employee of, or directly connected with, the audited centre.

8.4. The financial accounting information referred to in the three preceding Guidelines must be available on request to the Commonwealth through the relevant State commission and any problems concerning the delivery of this information to State commissions by a centre should be reported immediately to OLAA.

Internal accountability

9.1.   Centres must demonstrate that they are managing their affairs in a businesslike and systematic manner and keep appropriate records in pursuit of that objective. They must self test their own internal management arrangements and make any adjustments to ensure adequacy of administrative control. (Guideline 9.2 also refers.)

Accountability to community

9.2.   A centre must keep the community it serves informed of its operations, progress, plans and financial position on a regular basis.

Statistical and other reporting

9.3.   A centre must keep and make available such statistics as the State commissions or the Commonwealth may reasonably require, and report on all of its activities, and the perceived results of them, including activities that cannot easily be quantified or measured by statistical data (eg, community legal education projects).

Co-operation with other bodies

10.1.   In addition to satisfying the specific provisions outlined in these Guidelines, centres should, in general, co-operate and liaise with State commissions, other legal aid bodies and the Commonwealth.

Avoidance of duplication

10.2.   A centre should avoid any unnecessary duplication of services provided by other legal aid bodies.

Priorities for funding

11.1.   The Commonwealth has determined an order of priority which should be followed in recommending the allocation of available funds. This is specified at Guideline 11.3.

11.2.   It will be clear from the priority order that the Commonwealth does not, as a general policy, favour the making of 'seeding' grants to enable centres to commence operations. It has been longstanding policy that, in a situation of substantial and competing demands for funds, a centre should go at least part of the way towards demonstrating its viability and capabilities before qualifying for Commonwealth funding.

Index